T0035702

The
Animal
Atlas

A Pictorial Guide to the World's Wildlife

Illustrated by Kenneth Lilly

Written by Barbara Taylor

DK

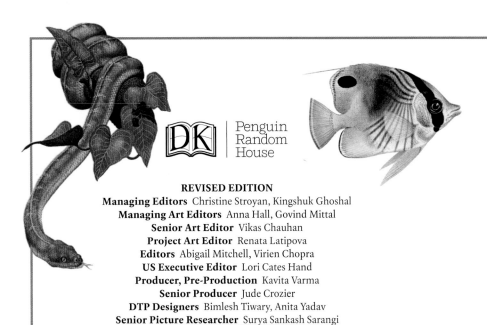

DK | Penguin Random House

REVISED EDITION
Managing Editors Christine Stroyan, Kingshuk Ghoshal
Managing Art Editors Anna Hall, Govind Mittal
Senior Art Editor Vikas Chauhan
Project Art Editor Renata Latipova
Editors Abigail Mitchell, Virien Chopra
US Executive Editor Lori Cates Hand
Producer, Pre-Production Kavita Varma
Senior Producer Jude Crozier
DTP Designers Bimlesh Tiwary, Anita Yadav
Senior Picture Researcher Surya Sankash Sarangi
Consultant Derek Harvey

FIRST EDITION
Project Editor Susan Peach **Art Editor** Richard Czapnik
Designer Marcus James **Production** Teresa Solomon
Managing Editor Ann Kramer **Art Director** Roger Priddy
Consultants Michael Chinery MA and Keith Lye BA, FRGS

This American Edition, 2020
First American Edition, 1992
Published in the United States by DK Publishing
1450 Broadway, Suite 801, New York, NY 10018

Copyright © 1992, 2020 Dorling Kindersley Limited
DK, a Division of Penguin Random House LLC
22 23 24 10 9 8 7 6 5 4 3 2
005–316676–May/2020

All rights reserved. Without limiting the rights under the copyright reserved
above, no part of this publication may be reproduced, stored in or introduced
into a retrieval system, or transmitted, in any form, or by any means (electronic,
mechanical, photocopying, recording, or otherwise), without the prior written
permission of the copyright owner.
Published in Great Britain by Dorling Kindersley Limited.

A catalog record for this book is available from the Library of Congress.
ISBN 978-1-4654-9097-1

DK books are available at special discounts when purchased
in bulk for sales promotions, premiums, fund-raising, or educational use.
For details, contact: DK Publishing Special Markets,
1450 Broadway, Suite 801, New York, NY 10018
SpecialSales@dk.com

Printed and bound in Malaysia

A WORLD OF IDEAS:
SEE ALL THERE IS TO KNOW

www.dk.com

CONTENTS

4 How to Use This Atlas

5 Animal Groups

6 Animal Habitats

8 The Arctic

NORTH AMERICA

10 Forests, Lakes, and Prairies

12 The Rockies

14 Western Deserts

16 The Everglades

18 Central America

SOUTH AMERICA

20 The Galápagos

22 The Andes

24 Amazon Rainforest

26 The Pampas

EUROPE

28 Conifer Forests

30 Woodlands

32 Southern Europe

AFRICA

34 The Sahara

36 Rainforests and Lakes

38 The Savannah

40 Madagascar

ASIA

42 Siberia

44 Deserts and Steppe

46 The Himalayas

48 The Far East

50 Southeastern Asia and India

AUSTRALASIA

52 The Outback

54 Rainforests and Woods

56 The Barrier Reef

57 Tasmania

58 New Zealand

59 Antarctica

60 Amazing Animals

62 Animals in Danger

64 Index

How to Use This Atlas

EACH DOUBLE-PAGE SPREAD in this atlas covers a particular type of habitat (the place where an animal lives). For example, the spread shown below is about European conifer forests. Habitats are arranged by continent, and there is a section in the book for each of the continents—North America, South America, Europe, Africa, Asia, Australasia, and Antarctica. The heading at the top of each page tells you which section you are in. Below you can see what the maps and symbols on each spread show, and what the abbreviations stand for.

Where on Earth?
This globe shows you where in the world the habitat featured on the spread is situated and its rough extent. On this page, for example, the red color shows the area covered by the European conifer forests.

Latin names

Wild cat (*Felis silvestris*)

Scientists have given each species of animal a Latin name, so that people all over the world can use the same name, no matter what language they speak. An animal's Latin name is divided into two parts. The first part is a group name given to a number of similar animals. For example, Felis is the group name given to all small cats. The second part of the name identifies the particular species of animal and often describes one of its specific characteristics. The full name for the wild cat shown here is *Felis silvestris*, which means "cat of the woods."

How big?

Length: up to 1.6 in (4 cm)

Labels next to each animal give the animal's vital statistics: its height, length, or wingspan. Like people, animals of the same species vary in size, so the measurement can only be approximate. Individual animals may be bigger or smaller than this size.

Scale
You can use this scale to figure out the size of the area shown on the map. The maps in the book have been drawn to different scales.

Animal symbols
The animal symbols on the map show the main area where the animals can be found, but some animals are widely distributed over the whole region. There is one symbol for each of the animals illustrated on the spread.

Map
The map shows the area of the habitat featured on the spread and surrounding regions. On these pages, for example, the map shows a large part of Europe, covering the conifer forests and the areas around them. The map also shows major geographic features in the region, and where the animals live. You can see the shape and position of the forests themselves on the globe in the top-left corner of the page.

Photos
The photographs around the map show you what the habitat looks like and what sort of vegetation can be found there.

ABBREVIATIONS USED IN THE BOOK	
mm millimeter	sq mile square mile
cm centimeter	kph kilometers per hour
in inch	mph miles per hour
m meter	kg kilogram
ft foot	lb pound
km kilometer	°C centigrade
sq km square kilometer	°F fahrenheit

Animal Groups

ABOUT A MILLION different kinds of animals have been discovered and described so far, but there are probably three or four times as many that people have never studied or named. Animals have several features in common. They move, breathe, feed, grow, have young, and respond to changes in their surroundings. To make animals easier to study, biologists divide them into a number of groups. The main groups are shown below.

Invertebrates

Invertebrates (animals without backbones) were the first animals to evolve on Earth, between 600 and 1,000 million years ago. Hundreds of thousands of species are alive today, and they far outnumber the vertebrates (animals with backbones). Invertebrates come in many different shapes and sizes, including corals, jellyfish, insects, snails, spiders, crabs, centipedes, and worms.

Monarch butterfly

Characteristic of invertebrates:

- do not have a backbone

Desert tarantula

Amphibians

Amphibians evolved from fishes more than 350 million years ago. There are more than 7,000 species alive today, including frogs, toads, and salamanders.

Characteristics of amphibians:

- adults live mainly on land, but breed in water
- cannot maintain a constant body temperature
- skin is usually soft with no scales
- life cycle is usually in three stages: egg, larva (or tadpole), and adult
- tadpoles breathe through gills at first; adults breathe through lungs

Japanese giant salamander

Green toad

Birds

Birds evolved from reptiles about 140 million years ago. There are more than 10,000 species alive today, including parrots, eagles, penguins, kiwis, owls, and storks. Most birds can fly. They are adapted for flight by having wings instead of front legs, a light skeleton with hollow bones, and a covering of feathers.

Kiwi

Characteristics of birds:

- birds are the only living animals with feathers
- breathe with lungs
- can maintain a constant body temperature
- lay eggs with hard, waterproof shells; usually incubate eggs with the heat of their bodies

Scarlet macaw

Fish

Fish were the first group of vertebrates to evolve from invertebrates about 500 million years ago. There are more than 30,000 species alive today—about the same as all the mammals, birds, reptiles, and amphibians put together. Examples include butterflyfish and sharks.

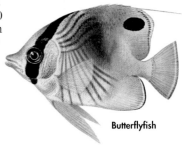

Butterflyfish

Characteristics of fish:

- adapted to live in water
- absorb oxygen from the water through gills; a few have lungs as well
- have fins to help them swim
- bodies are usually covered with scales

Blue shark

Reptiles

Reptiles evolved from amphibians about 300 million years ago. More than 10,000 species are alive today, including lizards, snakes, tortoises, turtles, and crocodiles. The dinosaurs were also reptiles.

Collared lizard

Characteristics of reptiles:

- cannot maintain a constant body temperature; may sleep through very hot or very cold weather
- have dry, scaly skin, sometimes with bony plates for protection
- most live and breed on land
- breathe with lungs

Western diamondback rattlesnake

Mammals

Mammals evolved from reptiles about 200 million years ago, during the age of the dinosaurs. There are nearly 6,000 species alive today, including kangaroos, rats, cats, elephants, whales, bats, monkeys, and humans.

Characteristics of mammals:

- mother feeds her young on milk
- bodies are covered with fur or hair
- can maintain a constant body temperature and have sweat glands to cool their bodies
- intelligent, with large brains
- breathe with lungs

Siberian tiger

Kangaroo rat

Animal Habitats

ANIMALS LIVE ALL OVER THE WORLD, from the frozen Arctic to hot deserts. The place where an animal lives is called its habitat. Many species can live together in the same habitat because they eat different kinds of food or make their homes in different places. The animal life in any habitat is a finely balanced mixture of species, and this balance can easily be disturbed.

The map on these two pages shows the main types of habitats around the world. Animals have adapted to live in each of these habitats by developing characteristics that help them survive. Similar types of habitats can be found in different parts of the world, and the animals that live there have

adapted in similar ways. For instance, the kit fox that lives in the North American deserts looks very similar to the fennec fox that lives in the Sahara Desert.

Physical barriers, such as mountains and seas, prevent many animals from moving freely from one place to another. Some, however, can fly or swim, so they spread over large areas. Tortoises, for example, can swim or float great distances across the sea.

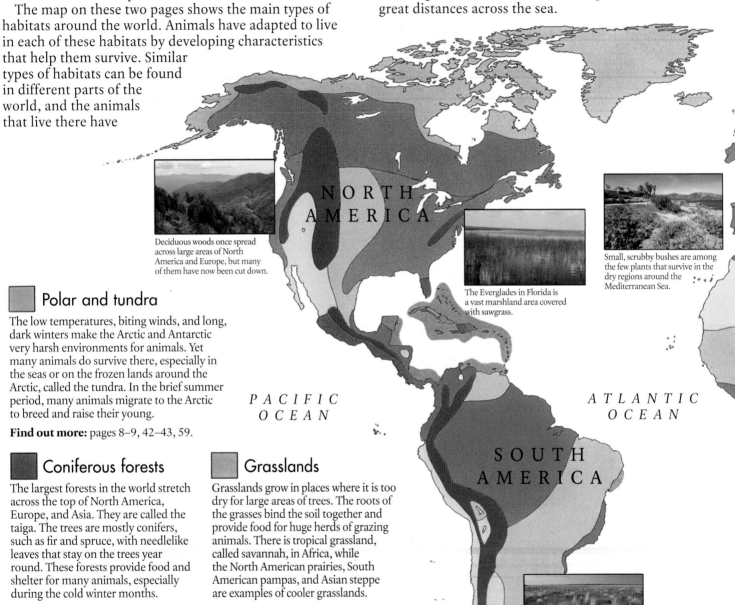

NORTH AMERICA

Deciduous woods once spread across large areas of North America and Europe, but many of them have now been cut down.

The Everglades in Florida is a vast marshland area covered with sawgrass.

Small, scrubby bushes are among the few plants that survive in the dry regions around the Mediterranean Sea.

PACIFIC OCEAN

ATLANTIC OCEAN

SOUTH AMERICA

The pampas is a huge area of grassland in South America. Much of it is used by farmers for grazing cattle.

A N T A R

 ## Polar and tundra

The low temperatures, biting winds, and long, dark winters make the Arctic and Antarctic very harsh environments for animals. Yet many animals do survive there, especially in the seas or on the frozen lands around the Arctic, called the tundra. In the brief summer period, many animals migrate to the Arctic to breed and raise their young.

Find out more: pages 8–9, 42–43, 59.

Coniferous forests

The largest forests in the world stretch across the top of North America, Europe, and Asia. They are called the taiga. The trees are mostly conifers, such as fir and spruce, with needlelike leaves that stay on the trees year round. These forests provide food and shelter for many animals, especially during the cold winter months.

Find out more: pages 10–11, 28–29, 42–43.

Deciduous woodlands

Deciduous woodlands are found south of the conifer forests, where the climate is mild and rainfall is plentiful throughout the year. The trees are mostly broadleaved species, such as oak and beech, which drop their leaves in the fall and rest over the cooler winter months.

Find out more: pages 10–11, 30–31.

 ## Grasslands

Grasslands grow in places where it is too dry for large areas of trees. The roots of the grasses bind the soil together and provide food for huge herds of grazing animals. There is tropical grassland, called savannah, in Africa, while the North American prairies, South American pampas, and Asian steppe are examples of cooler grasslands.

Find out more: pages 10–11, 26–27, 38–39, 44–45.

Scrubland

Dusty, dry land dotted with tough shrubs and small trees is found around the Mediterranean Sea, in Australia, and in California in the United States. Most rain falls in the winter months, and animals that live in these regions adapt to survive the dry, hot summers.

Find out more: pages 32–33.

Deserts

It hardly ever rains in the deserts, so the animals that live there have to survive without drinking for long periods or get all the water they need from their food. They also have to cope with boiling-hot days and freezing-cold nights. Many animals come out only at dawn and dusk when it is cooler and more humid.

Find out more: pages 14–15, 34–35, 44–45, 52–53.

Rainforests

Rainforests grow near the equator, where the weather is warm and humid year round. Most of the trees are evergreen with broad leaves. Rainforests contain the richest variety of wildlife to be found anywhere on Earth. More than 50 percent of all the different kinds of plants and animals in the world live in the rainforests.

Find out more: pages 24–25, 36–37, 54–55.

Marshes and swamp

Marshy, waterlogged places develop near lakes and rivers and along coasts. One of the largest marshland areas is the Everglades in Florida. Mangrove swamps often fringe the coasts in tropical areas. Both these habitats are rich in food supplies and places to breed, and provide homes for a wide variety of animals, especially birds and insects.

Find out more: pages 16–17.

Mountains

Mountains are found in both warm and cold regions of the world. They provide a wide range of habitats for wildlife, from forests on the lower slopes to grassland and tundra farther up. The higher up you go, the colder it becomes. Above a certain height—called the tree line—the temperature is too low for trees to survive. Even higher up is the snow line. Above this it is so cold that the ground is always covered in snow and ice. The climate in mountainous regions can be severe, with low temperatures, fierce winds, and low rainfall. Mountain animals also have to cope with steep, slippery slopes.

Find out more: pages 12–13, 22–23, 46–47.

A huge area of coniferous trees—the largest forest in the world—stretches across northern Asia.

E U R O P E

M E D I T E R R A N E A N   S E A

A S I A

A F R I C A

The biggest coral reef on Earth is the Great Barrier Reef, off the coast of northeastern Australia.

Mount Kilimanjaro in Africa lies almost on the equator, but it is so high that its peak is covered in snow.

P A C I F I C
O C E A N

I N D I A N
O C E A N

Rainforests are packed with dense jungle vegetation and are home to a wide variety of animals.

A U S T R A L A S I A

The central part of Australia—called the outback—consists of dry, rocky deserts where few plants can grow.

Coral reefs

Coral reefs are made of the skeletons of tiny creatures called corals. Over millions of years they build up on top of one another to form a reef. Reefs develop only in warm, shallow, salty water. A huge variety of fish, corals, sponges, and other animals lives on a reef.

Find out more: page 56.

Antarctica is the coldest and most isolated continent on Earth. A thick ice cap covers most of the land.

C T I C A

The Arctic

THE ARCTIC consists of the northernmost parts of North America, Europe, and Asia, which is tundra (frozen land), and a huge area of frozen ocean around the North Pole. It is one of the coldest places on Earth. The temperature rarely rises above 50°F (10°C), and in the winter it often drops to −40°F (−40°C). During the brief summer period, it is light for 24 hours a day. Light and warmth encourage the growth of tiny sea animals and plants called plankton, which are eaten by fish, seals, and birds. On land, flowers bloom, providing food for millions of insects. Many birds migrate to the Arctic to breed and raise their young. When the winter sets in again, these birds return to warmer climates.

Food store
During the summer the Arctic fox stores food, such as dead birds, under rocks. Thanks to the cold climate, this food keeps as well as it would in a refrigerator. The fox eats it in the winter months, when fresh food is hard to find. The fox's thick fur coat helps it survive in temperatures as low as −58°F (−50°C).

Arctic fox
(*Alopex lagopus*)
Body length: up to
2 ft 5 in (75 cm)
Tail: up to 16.7 in
(42.5 cm)

Wonderful whiskers
The bearded seal lives in the seas around the edge of the ice cap. It has long, sensitive whiskers, which it uses to feel for shellfish on the sea bed. In spring, the female hauls herself onto the ice to give birth.

Polar bear
(*Ursus maritimus*)
Height at shoulder: up to 4 ft 11 in (1.5 m)
Body length: up to 9 ft 7 in (2.9 m)

Bearded seal
(*Erignathus barbatus*)
Length: up to 8 ft 2 in (2.5 m)

Reindeer warble-fly
(*Hypoderma tarandi*)
Length: up to 0.7 in
(1.8 cm)

Hooded seal
(*Cystophora cristata*)
Length: up to
8 ft 10 in (2.7 m)

Fearsome fly
The reindeer warble-fly lays its eggs in the fur of caribou and reindeer, which migrate to the Arctic in summer. When the eggs hatch, the grubs burrow through the skin and live in the deer's flesh. The grubs later fall off and grow into adults.

Balloon nose
The male hooded seal has a strange balloonlike structure on the end of his nose. In the breeding season, he blows air into this structure, which can become 12 in (30 cm) long. The air amplifies the loud calls he makes to warn off other males. The hooded seal spends most of its life at sea, searching for fish and squid. It only comes out onto the ice to mate, breed, and molt.

Lethal paws
The polar bear is a huge animal and can weigh as much as 10 adult people. It feeds mainly on seals, and often catches them at holes in the ice when they come up for air. One swipe from the bear's massive paws can kill a seal, and its claws then grab and hold onto its prey.

Longest hair
The musk ox has the longest coat of almost any mammal. Some hairs in its outer coat are nearly 3 ft 3 in (1 m) long. If a group of musk oxen are attacked, they form a tight circle and defend themselves with their sharp horns, while the young stand in the middle for protection.

Musk ox
(*Ovibos moschatus*)
Height at shoulder: up to 5 ft (1.5 m)

Narwhal
(*Monodon monoceros*)
Body length: up to 16 ft 9 in (5 m)
Tusk: up to 9 ft 10 in (3 m)

Arctic unicorn
The narwhal is a mammal related to whales and dolphins. It has only two teeth. One of the male's teeth grows into a long, spiraling tusk, which sticks out through a hole in his top lip. The tusks are used to display dominance, and males have been seen fighting one another with their tusks.

Champion migrator

The Arctic tern raises its chicks in the Arctic during the brief summer period. Then it flies 8,000 miles (13,000 km) to Antarctica to take advantage of the summer months there when plenty of food is available. This is the longest migration route of any bird. An Arctic tern can live for 30 years or more, so it may travel more than 500,000 miles (800,000 km) in its lifetime.

Arctic tern
(*Sterna paradisaea*)
Length: up to 14 in (36 cm)

Sea canary

Beluga or white whales communicate with each other using a variety of songs, leading 19th-century sailors to know them as "sea canaries." They also make clicking noises that bounce off objects around them and help them find their way around. In winter, beluga whales gather together in huge herds and migrate south.

Beluga whale
(*Delphinapterus leucas*)
Length: up to 14 ft 9 in (4.5 m)

Mountain hare
(*Lepus timidus*)
Body length: up to 1 ft 10 in (55 cm)
Tail: up to 2.5 in (6.5 cm)

Few animals live on the frozen polar ice cap, as there are no plants or insects to provide food.

Areas of the Arctic that are not permanently covered in ice are known as tundra, which is frozen under the surface.

Much of the island of Greenland is covered in flowing rivers of ice, called glaciers.

Map labels
NORTH AMERICA
MUSK OX
BEAUFORT SEA
BELUGA WHALE
ARCTIC CIRCLE
ASIA
REINDEER WARBLE-FLY
BANK ISLAND
Lena
Olenëk
COMMON EIDER
POLAR BEAR
LAPTEV SEA
ARCTIC OCEAN
• NORTH POLE
ARCTIC TERN
ARCTIC FOX
ELLESMERE ISLAND
BAFFIN ISLAND
MOUNTAIN HARE
BEARDED SEAL
NARWHAL
WALRUS
GREENLAND
HOODED SEAL
ATLANTIC OCEAN
ICELAND
NORWEGIAN SEA

KILOMETERS
0 300 600 900
0 300 600
MILES

Changing color

The Mountain hare can change the color of its coat to match its surroundings. In the winter, its fur is white and gray. This makes it hard to see against the snow. In spring, when the snow melts, the hare sheds its white fur and grows a brown coat.

Common eider
(*Somateria mollissima*)
Length: up to 2 ft 4 in (71 cm)

Island nests

The common eider duck breeds among clumps of grass on small islands in the Arctic Ocean. These remote nesting sites help protect the young. The female bird plucks soft down feathers from her breast and uses them to line the nest. If the parent birds have to leave the nest, they pull the down over the eggs. This keeps the eggs warm and helps hide them from enemies, such as gulls and foxes.

Walrus
(*Odobenus rosmarus*)
Length: up to 11 ft 5 in (3.5 m)
Tusks: up to 39 in (100 cm)

Digging teeth

The walrus has long tusks, which it uses to dig up shellfish and other small animals from the sea bed. Walruses live in large groups and spend much of the day sleeping. In the breeding season, walruses gather together and males compete against each other to win mates.

Forests, Lakes, and Prairies

THE EVERGREEN FORESTS OF CANADA consist of dense areas of spruce, pine, and fir trees. These forests are marshy underfoot, with many lakes. Farther south, forests of oak, hickory, and chestnut trees once spread across the eastern part of North America, but today, vast areas have been destroyed for lumber or farming. Some forest animals, such as the raccoon and the opossum, have adapted to this new environment, but many have declined in number or retreated to the hills. The prairies once formed a huge sea of grass. Millions of bison and pronghorn antelope once grazed there, but they were almost wiped out by hunters in the 19th century.

Raccoon
(*Procyon lotor*)
Body length:
up to 2 ft (62 cm)
Tail: up to 14 in (36 cm)

Trash raider

The raccoon has long, sensitive fingers that it uses to search for food. It often comes into cities and raids trash cans for leftover food scraps. The raccoon's thick fur coat keeps it warm during cold winter months.

Sage grouse
(*Centrocercus urophasianus*)
Length: up to 30 in (76 cm)

Big cheeks

The least chipmunk has large cheek pouches, which it uses to carry food back to its underground burrow. Inside the burrow are chambers used for storing food, living, and nesting. During winter, the chipmunk hibernates in its home.

Sage smells

The sage grouse feeds on the leaves of the sagebrush plant. Eventually its flesh takes on a strong sage flavor. During the spring, the male puts on a special display to win a mate. He puffs out his chest feathers, opens and closes his tail, and inflates the air sacs on his neck, which make loud booming, popping noises.

Two-spotted ladybug
(*Adalia bipunctata*)
Length: up to 0.25 in (6 mm)

Pest control

The two-spotted ladybug is common throughout North America and can be found in forests, fields, and gardens. It feeds on small insects and helps keep down the number of pests in gardens and fields. The ladybug's hard, red wing cases protect its soft wings and body underneath.

Least chipmunk
(*Tamias minimus*)
Body length: up to 4.5 in (11.4 cm)
Tail: up to 3.3 in (8.5 cm)

Yukon BALD EAGLE MOOSE

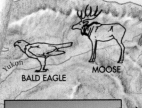

The forest lakes are home to many water birds, including gulls, ducks, and swans.

Bugle bird

Named for its bugle-like call, the whooping crane nests only in a remote area of northwest Canada. By the 1940s it had been almost wiped out by hunting. It is now a protected species.

Moose (*Alces alces*)
Height at shoulder: up to 6 ft 10 in (2.1 m)
Length: up to 10 ft 4 in (3.2 m)

Heavyweight deer

The moose is the largest deer in the world. In the fall, a male may weigh more than 1,000 lbs (450 kg). The moose's broad hooves and long legs help it travel through deep snow, bogs, or lakes. Its overhanging top lip enables the moose to tear off leaves and branches. The male uses his antlers to fight other males and win mates.

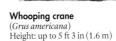

Whooping crane
(*Grus americana*)
Height: up to 5 ft 3 in (1.6 m)
Wingspan: up to 7 ft 6 in (2.3 m)

Today the flat plains of the prairies are used for growing wheat.

Barking burrower

The prairie dog is a type of squirrel that lives in networks of tunnels under the prairies. Its name comes from the barking noise it makes when it is alarmed. Before people started to farm the region, prairie dog colonies covered vast areas with millions of inhabitants.

Black-tailed prairie dog
(*Cynomys ludovicianus*)
Body length: up to 15 in (38 cm)
Tail: up to 3.5 in (9 cm)

White head

The bald eagle gets its name from its white head—an old meaning of the word "bald" is "white." Bald eagles have spectacular courtship displays, in which the male and the female bird lock talons in flight and somersault through the air. Pairs build a huge nest of sticks, weeds, and soil and add to it each year.

Bald eagle
(*Haliaeetus leucocephalus*)
Length: up to 3 ft 2 in (96 cm)
Wingspan: up to 8 ft (2.4 m)

Monarch butterfly
(*Danaus plexippus*)
Wingspan: up to 4.9 in (12.5 cm)

Dam builder

The beaver has powerful jaws and strong front teeth, which it uses to gnaw through tree trunks. The beaver then builds a dam across a river, and a lodge of sticks and mud in the pond that forms.

Terrific traveler

In fall, the monarch butterfly migrates from Canada to California, Mexico, or the Caribbean—flying more than 2,000 miles (3,200 km). It travels north again in the spring, but stops on the way to mate and then die.

North American beaver (*Castor canadensis*)
Body length: up to 2 ft 11 in (90 cm)
Tail: up to 12 in (30 cm)

Wolverine (*Gulo gulo*)
Height at shoulder: up to 17 in (43 cm)
Body length: up to 3 ft 5 in (105 cm)

Crushing bite

Known to kill animals as large as a caribou, the fierce wolverine is strong for its size, with a powerful, crushing bite. Its widespread toes help it bound across snow chasing its prey. A wolverine can travel over 40 miles (65 km) without resting.

Blue jay
(*Cyanocitta cristata*)
Length: 11.8 in (30 cm)

Great Bear Lake

Mackenzie

WHOOPING CRANE

WOLVERINE

Great Slave Lake

Aerial view of fall trees in the deciduous forests of New England.

Peace

TWO-SPOTTED LADYBUG

HUDSON BAY

N O R T H

Lake Winnipeg

LEAST CHIPMUNK

RACCOON

BLUE JAY

MONARCH BUTTERFLY

Missouri

St. Lawrence

A M E R I C A

GREAT LAKES

SAGE GROUSE

Snake

Great Salt Lake

VIRGINIA OPOSSUM

NORTH AMERICAN BEAVER

Colorado

BLACK-TAILED PRAIRIE DOG

Arkansas

Mississippi

APPALACHIAN MTS

ATLANTIC OCEAN

Red

Rio Grande

KILOMETERS
0   400   800   1200

0   400   800
MILES

Tree planter

The blue jay often buries acorns and other tree seeds to eat later. Some survive to grow into new trees, helping the forest spread. In spring and fall, large flocks of blue jays migrate south to warmer climates.

Virginia opossum
(*Didelphis virginiana*)
Body length: up to 19.6 in (50 cm)
Tail: up to 18.5 in (47 cm)

Baby pouch

The opossum is North America's only pouched mammal. The young climb into the mother's pouch after birth and stay there for several months, feeding on her milk. To escape an enemy, opossums can "play dead," and may stay in a trancelike state for hours.

The Rockies

THE ROCKIES ARE A VAST range of mountains that stretch down the western side of North America. The Rockies form a barrier to the moist winds that sweep toward the continent from the Pacific Ocean. As these winds rise up over the mountains and cool, the water they carry falls as rain or snow. On the mountain peaks, winds can reach 200 mph (320 kph) and temperatures may fall to –60°F (–51°C). The Rockies provide a refuge for animals that have been hunted or driven out of other habitats by people. Some species are specially adapted for climbing and jumping on the mountain slopes. Many animals have warm fur to protect them against the cold and the winds.

Rocky Mountain parnassian
(*Parnassius sminthius*)
Wingspan: up to 2.6 in (6.8 cm)

Summer butterfly

Male phoebus butterflies appear in the Rockies in mid-summer. They fly across the meadows to find the females, which emerge eight to ten days later.

Spiky armor

The porcupine's furry coat hides about 30,000 spiky hairs, called quills. When threatened, the porcupine turns its back, raises its quills, and lashes its tail. Its barbed tail quills stick into an enemy's skin.

North American porcupine
(*Erethizon dorsatum*)
Body length: up to 4 ft 4 in (1.3 m)
Tail: up to 9.8 in (25 cm)

Grizzled giant

The huge grizzly bear gets its name from the whitish (grizzled) tips of its hair. It can kill an animal as large as a moose or caribou, but usually feeds on smaller animals, fish, and plants. A grizzly can run as fast as a horse for short distances and may stand up on its back legs to get a better view of its prey, which it kills with its long front claws. In fall, the grizzly eats as much as possible to build up stores of fat to last it through its winter hibernation.

Grizzly bear
(*Ursus arctos horribilis*)
Total length: up to 9 ft 10 in (3 m)

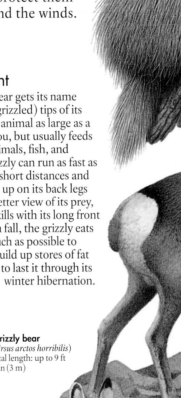

Nonskid feet

The bighorn sheep is good at climbing the steep mountain slopes. Each of its hooves is divided into two halves that separate to help the sheep grip the rocks. The male uses its curving horns to fight rivals in the breeding season.

Bighorn sheep (*Ovis canadensis*)
Body length: up to 5 ft 6 in (1.7 m)
Horns: up to 4 ft 1 in (126 cm)

Winter white

In summer the snowshoe hare has brown fur, but in winter it grows a white coat for camouflage against the snow. It also develops dense fur on its feet, which stop it from sinking into the snow.

Snowshoe hare
(*Lepus americanus*)
Length: up to 23 in (58 cm)

Spotted camouflage

The bobcat's spotted coat helps it blend in with its environment, so that it can creep up on its prey. It usually feeds on rabbits and hares, but will eat almost any reptile, mammal, or bird. It can even kill a deer, providing enough food for a week or more.

Bobcat (*Lynx rufus*)
Height at shoulder: 22.8 in (58 cm) Length: up to 3 ft 9 in (1.2 m)

Tree glider

The northern flying squirrel glides from tree to tree using flaps of skin along the sides of its body that unfold like wings. It can glide up to 125 ft (38 m), moving its legs and using its tail to change direction.

Northern flying squirrel
(*Glaucomys sabrinus*)
Body length: up to 7.5 in (19 cm)
Tail: up to 6.3 in (16 cm)

Rocky Mountain goat
(*Oreamnos americanus*)
Height to shoulder:
up to 3 ft 7 in (1.1 m)

Clinging toes

The Rocky Mountain goat has curved toes, which help it cling to steep slopes and rocky crags where it is safe from most enemies. A baby goat can stand minutes after birth, and can follow its mother over the steep slopes within days.

Insect catcher

The mountain bluebird eats seeds, berries, and insects. It darts out from a perch to snatch any insects flying past or flies low to pounce on prey on the ground.

Prowling pouncer

The puma (also called the mountain lion or cougar) stalks its prey at night. It creeps up on its victim and then pounces on it from an overhanging tree or rock. Long, sharp claws help the mountain lion hold its prey, which it kills by biting through the neck.

Mountain bluebird
(*Sialia currucoides*)
Length: up to 7.8 in (20 cm)

White-tailed ptarmigan
(*Lagopus leucura*)
Length: up to 13.4 in (34 cm)

Puma (*Puma concolor*)
Height at shoulder: up to 2 ft 3 in (70 cm)
Body length: up to 7 ft 10 in (2.4 m)

Feathered feet

The ptarmigan's feathered feet keep it warm and keep it from sinking into the snow. During the breeding season, the female's striped feathers camouflage her on the nest. In winter both the male and female grow white feathers to hide them on the snow.

Up to 200 ft (60 m) of snow may fall on the Rockies each year.

Many of North America's great rivers, such as the Missouri, start in the Rockies.

The slopes of the Rockies are covered by fir and pine trees.

Wapiti
(*Cervus canadensis*)
Height at shoulder:
5 ft 6 in (1.6 m)
Antlers: up to 5 ft 5 in (1.6 m)

Amazing antlers

The wapiti is a type of deer. During the fall breeding season, the males fight one another with their huge antlers to win mates. A male's antlers can weigh up to 25 lbs (11 kg). The name wapiti comes from the American Indian word for "white," and refers to the white patch on the animal's rear.

ARCTIC OCEAN

Great Bear Lake

Great Slave Lake

GRIZZLY BEAR

WHITE-TAILED PTARMIGAN

NORTHERN FLYING SQUIRREL

SNOWSHOE HARE

ROCKY MOUNTAIN GOAT

BIGHORN SHEEP

Lake Winnipeg

GULF OF ALASKA

NORTH

NORTH AMERICAN PORCUPINE

AMERICA

PACIFIC OCEAN

WAPITI

ROCKY MOUNTAIN PARNASSIAN

MOUNTAIN BLUEBIRD

BOBCAT

GREAT PLAINS

Great Salt Lake

Missouri

PUMA

KILOMETERS
0   250   500   750

0   250   500
MILES

COAST RANGES

SIERRA NEVADA

Colorado

Yukon

Western Deserts

THE STONY DESERTS OF NORTH AMERICA cover large areas of the southwestern United States and northern Mexico. The largest is the Great Basin, which is sandwiched between two ranges of mountains—the Rockies to the east and the Sierras to the west. To the south, the Great Basin merges with the Mojave Desert. Between the two lies Death Valley, one of the hottest places on Earth. South of the Mojave is the Sonoran Desert, which is famous for its giant saguaro cacti.

The desert is a harsh environment, but many animals survive there, making the most of the little moisture available. Some survive without drinking at all. Many stay in burrows during the day, emerging only at night when the air is cooler and damper.

Warning rattle

The western diamondback rattlesnake has a "rattle" on its tail, which scares away animals that might step on it. The rattle is made up of loose rings of hard skin, one of which is left behind when the snake sheds its skin. Rattlesnakes are venomous and kill small animals by striking them with their long fangs.

Western diamondback rattlesnake (*Crotalus atrox*)
Length: up to 7 ft (2.1 m)

Desert swallowtail
(*Papilio polyxenes coloro*)
Wingspan: up to 3.5 in (9 cm)

Antenna ears

The kit fox is the smallest fox in North America. It comes out at night to hunt, using its huge ears as antennae to track down its prey, which is mainly kangaroo rats, prairie dogs, and rabbits. The fox is able to run very swiftly to overtake and seize them before they disappear down their burrows.

Kit fox (*Vulpes macrotis*)
Body length: up to 21 in (53.5 cm)
Tail: up to 13 in (34 cm)

Smelly defense

A spotted skunk protects itself from its enemies by spraying them with a foul-smelling liquid. This comes from scent glands under its tail. The skunk can hit a target accurately from 3.6 m (12 ft) away. Before it sprays, the skunk stands on its hands to display its striking black and white fur as a warning. The skunk comes out mainly at night to hunt for small animals, eggs, insects, and fruit.

Trailing tails

The desert swallowtail butterfly is named after the long, trailing tails on its back wings, which resemble a swallow's tail. It lives in the mountain canyons of the desert, and only breeds after it rains. The caterpillars of this butterfly give off a foul smell if they are disturbed. This helps frighten off enemies.

Western spotted skunk
(*Spilogale gracilis*)
Body length: up to 14.5 in (37 cm)
Tail: up to 8 in (21 cm)

Cactus wren
(*Campylorhynchus brunneicapillus*)
Length: up to 7.5 in (19 cm)

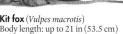

Spiny fortress

The cactus wren builds a large, domed nest among the spines of a cactus or a thorny bush to keep its young safe from enemies. The bird's tough feathers and hard, scaly legs protect it from scratches. The wren may also build extra nests to roost in during the winter.

Roadrunner
(*Geococcyx californianus*)
Length: up to 1 ft 10 in (58 cm)

Speedy bird

The roadrunner lives on the ground and rarely flies. It has very powerful legs and can run at speeds of up to 15 mph (24 kph). Its long tail helps it swerve suddenly or come to a sharp halt. The roadrunner is very strong, and can kill a snake with one bite from its sharp beak.

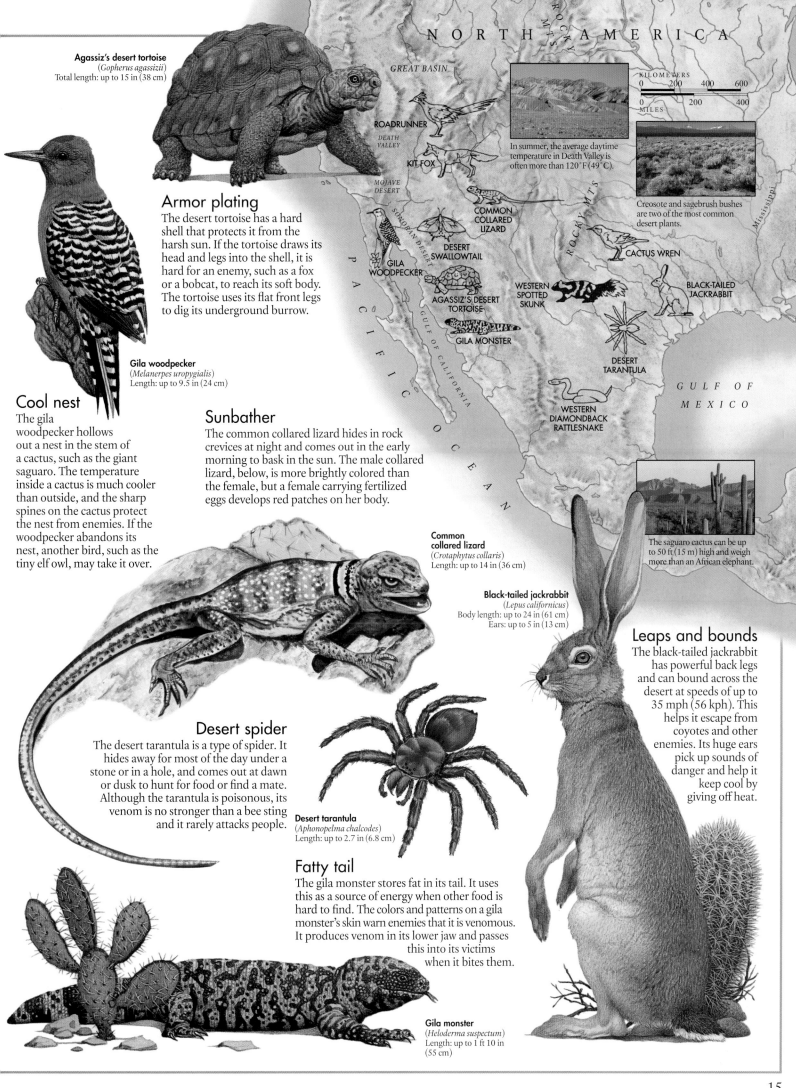

Agassiz's desert tortoise
(*Gopherus agassizii*)
Total length: up to 15 in (38 cm)

GREAT BASIN

ROADRUNNER

DEATH VALLEY

KIT FOX

MOJAVE DESERT

In summer, the average daytime temperature in Death Valley is often more than 120°F (49°C).

KILOMETERS
0   200   400   600
0   200   400
MILES

COMMON COLLARED LIZARD

DESERT SWALLOWTAIL

GILA WOODPECKER

AGASSIZ'S DESERT TORTOISE

GILA MONSTER

WESTERN SPOTTED SKUNK

Creosote and sagebrush bushes are two of the most common desert plants.

CACTUS WREN

BLACK-TAILED JACKRABBIT

DESERT TARANTULA

GULF OF MEXICO

WESTERN DIAMONDBACK RATTLESNAKE

ROCKY MTS

SONORAN DESERT

GULF OF CALIFORNIA

PACIFIC OCEAN

Mississippi

Armor plating

The desert tortoise has a hard shell that protects it from the harsh sun. If the tortoise draws its head and legs into the shell, it is hard for an enemy, such as a fox or a bobcat, to reach its soft body. The tortoise uses its flat front legs to dig its underground burrow.

Gila woodpecker
(*Melanerpes uropygialis*)
Length: up to 9.5 in (24 cm)

Cool nest

The gila woodpecker hollows out a nest in the stem of a cactus, such as the giant saguaro. The temperature inside a cactus is much cooler than outside, and the sharp spines on the cactus protect the nest from enemies. If the woodpecker abandons its nest, another bird, such as the tiny elf owl, may take it over.

Sunbather

The common collared lizard hides in rock crevices at night and comes out in the early morning to bask in the sun. The male collared lizard, below, is more brightly colored than the female, but a female carrying fertilized eggs develops red patches on her body.

Common collared lizard
(*Crotaphytus collaris*)
Length: up to 14 in (36 cm)

The saguaro cactus can be up to 50 ft (15 m) high and weigh more than an African elephant.

Black-tailed jackrabbit
(*Lepus californicus*)
Body length: up to 24 in (61 cm)
Ears: up to 5 in (13 cm)

Desert spider

The desert tarantula is a type of spider. It hides away for most of the day under a stone or in a hole, and comes out at dawn or dusk to hunt for food or find a mate. Although the tarantula is poisonous, its venom is no stronger than a bee sting and it rarely attacks people.

Desert tarantula
(*Aphonopelma chalcodes*)
Length: up to 2.7 in (6.8 cm)

Leaps and bounds

The black-tailed jackrabbit has powerful back legs and can bound across the desert at speeds of up to 35 mph (56 kph). This helps it escape from coyotes and other enemies. Its huge ears pick up sounds of danger and help it keep cool by giving off heat.

Fatty tail

The gila monster stores fat in its tail. It uses this as a source of energy when other food is hard to find. The colors and patterns on a gila monster's skin warn enemies that it is venomous. It produces venom in its lower jaw and passes this into its victims when it bites them.

Gila monster
(*Heloderma suspectum*)
Length: up to 1 ft 10 in (55 cm)

The Everglades

THE SEMITROPICAL MARSHLAND of Everglades National Park covers 2,120 sq miles (5,490 sq km) of southern Florida in the United States. The Everglades is an enormous swamp with deeper channels of water running through it. Grass covers most of the swamp, broken only by islands of trees. There are two main seasons in the Everglades: the wet summer and the dry winter. The park provides a rich feeding and breeding ground for large numbers of insects, fish, reptiles, and birds. However, the Everglades is threatened by population increase, agriculture, pollution, and canal construction, which have all disrupted the natural flow of water. Only two percent of the habitat is intact.

Loggerhead turtle
(*Caretta caretta*)
Length: up to 7 ft (2.1 m)

Dangerous journey

The female loggerhead turtle comes ashore at night to lay her eggs on the beach. She digs a hole, lays more than a hundred eggs, covers them with sand, and returns to the sea. After about eight weeks, the baby turtles hatch out and make their way as quickly as they can to the safety of the water. Many of them are eaten by sea birds before they can get there.

American alligator
(*Alligator mississippiensis*)
Length: up to 14 ft 4 in (4.4 m)

Poisonous butterfly

The caterpillar of the zebra butterfly feeds on passion flower vines, which are poisonous to most animals. Adult butterflies build up poison by feeding on pollens.

Everglade kite
(*Rostrhamus sociabilis*)
Length: up to 19 in (48 cm)
Wingspan: 3 ft 9 in (1.1 m)

Zebra butterfly (*Heliconius charithonia*)
Wingspan: up to 4 in (10 cm)

Hole maker

American alligators clean out large holes in the swamp floor. During the dry season, when the Everglades dry up, these holes stay filled with water. The alligators then feed on the turtles, garfish, and other animals that take refuge there.

Islands of trees, called hammocks, stick up above the water level.

Snail diet

The snail kite (also called an Everglade kite) is named for its diet: it mostly eats only one type of water snail, called *Pomacea*. The kite uses its slender, hooked beak to pry out the snail's soft body without breaking its shell. Everglade kites nest in huge colonies and search for food in groups.

Water snake

The cottonmouth snake, a pit viper, has pits (holes) on its face that can sense heat. It hunts at night, killing frogs and fish with its venomous fangs. This is the only viper that is equally at home in the water as it is on land, and is also known as the water moccasin.

Super diver

The brown pelican feeds on fish. It catches its prey by diving into the sea and scooping up a mouthful of fish and water in the huge pouch under its beak. Often this water weighs twice as much as the bird itself. A brown pelican can scoop up a fish in less than two seconds.

Brown pelican (*Pelecanus occidentalis*)
Length: up to 4 ft 11 in (1.5 m)
Wingspan: up to 7 ft 5 in (2.3 m)

Cottonmouth
(*Agkistrodon piscivorus*)
Length: up to 6 ft (1.8 m)

BOUNDARY OF EVERGLADES
NATIONAL PARK

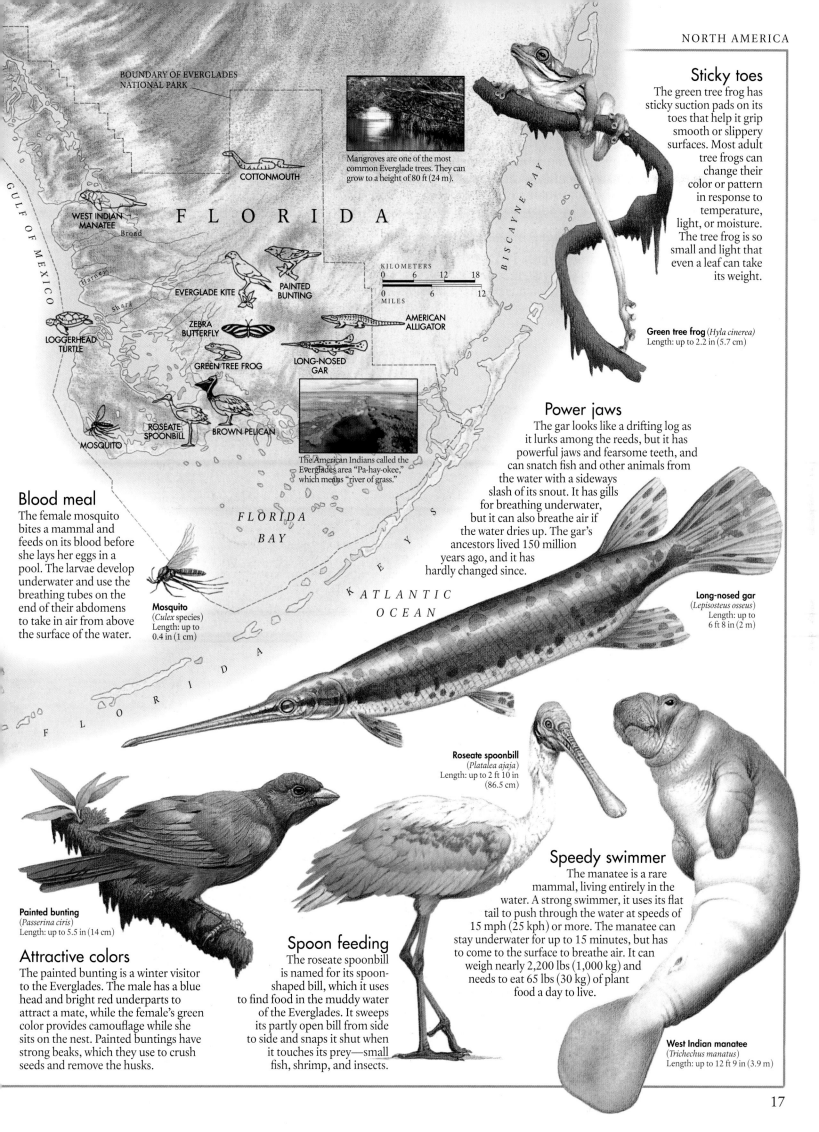

Mangroves are one of the most common Everglade trees. They can grow to a height of 80 ft (24 m).

COTTONMOUTH

F L O R I D A

GULF OF MEXICO

WEST INDIAN MANATEE

Broad

Harney

EVERGLADE KITE

PAINTED BUNTING

Shark

LOGGERHEAD TURTLE

ZEBRA BUTTERFLY

GREEN TREE FROG

LONG-NOSED GAR

AMERICAN ALLIGATOR

ROSEATE SPOONBILL

BROWN PELICAN

MOSQUITO

KILOMETERS
0   6   12   18
0   6   12
MILES

BISCAYNE BAY

The American Indians called the Everglades area "Pa-hay-okee," which means "river of grass."

F L O R I D A   B A Y

F L O R I D A   K E Y S

A T L A N T I C   O C E A N

Sticky toes

The green tree frog has sticky suction pads on its toes that help it grip smooth or slippery surfaces. Most adult tree frogs can change their color or pattern in response to temperature, light, or moisture. The tree frog is so small and light that even a leaf can take its weight.

Green tree frog (*Hyla cinerea*)
Length: up to 2.2 in (5.7 cm)

Power jaws

The gar looks like a drifting log as it lurks among the reeds, but it has powerful jaws and fearsome teeth, and can snatch fish and other animals from the water with a sideways slash of its snout. It has gills for breathing underwater, but it can also breathe air if the water dries up. The gar's ancestors lived 150 million years ago, and it has hardly changed since.

Long-nosed gar (*Lepisosteus osseus*)
Length: up to 6 ft 8 in (2 m)

Blood meal

The female mosquito bites a mammal and feeds on its blood before she lays her eggs in a pool. The larvae develop underwater and use the breathing tubes on the end of their abdomens to take in air from above the surface of the water.

Mosquito (*Culex* species)
Length: up to 0.4 in (1 cm)

Roseate spoonbill (*Platalea ajaja*)
Length: up to 2 ft 10 in (86.5 cm)

Attractive colors

The painted bunting is a winter visitor to the Everglades. The male has a blue head and bright red underparts to attract a mate, while the female's green color provides camouflage while she sits on the nest. Painted buntings have strong beaks, which they use to crush seeds and remove the husks.

Painted bunting (*Passerina ciris*)
Length: up to 5.5 in (14 cm)

Spoon feeding

The roseate spoonbill is named for its spoon-shaped bill, which it uses to find food in the muddy water of the Everglades. It sweeps its partly open bill from side to side and snaps it shut when it touches its prey—small fish, shrimp, and insects.

Speedy swimmer

The manatee is a rare mammal, living entirely in the water. A strong swimmer, it uses its flat tail to push through the water at speeds of 15 mph (25 kph) or more. The manatee can stay underwater for up to 15 minutes, but has to come to the surface to breathe air. It can weigh nearly 2,200 lbs (1,000 kg) and needs to eat 65 lbs (30 kg) of plant food a day to live.

West Indian manatee (*Trichechus manatus*)
Length: up to 12 ft 9 in (3.9 m)

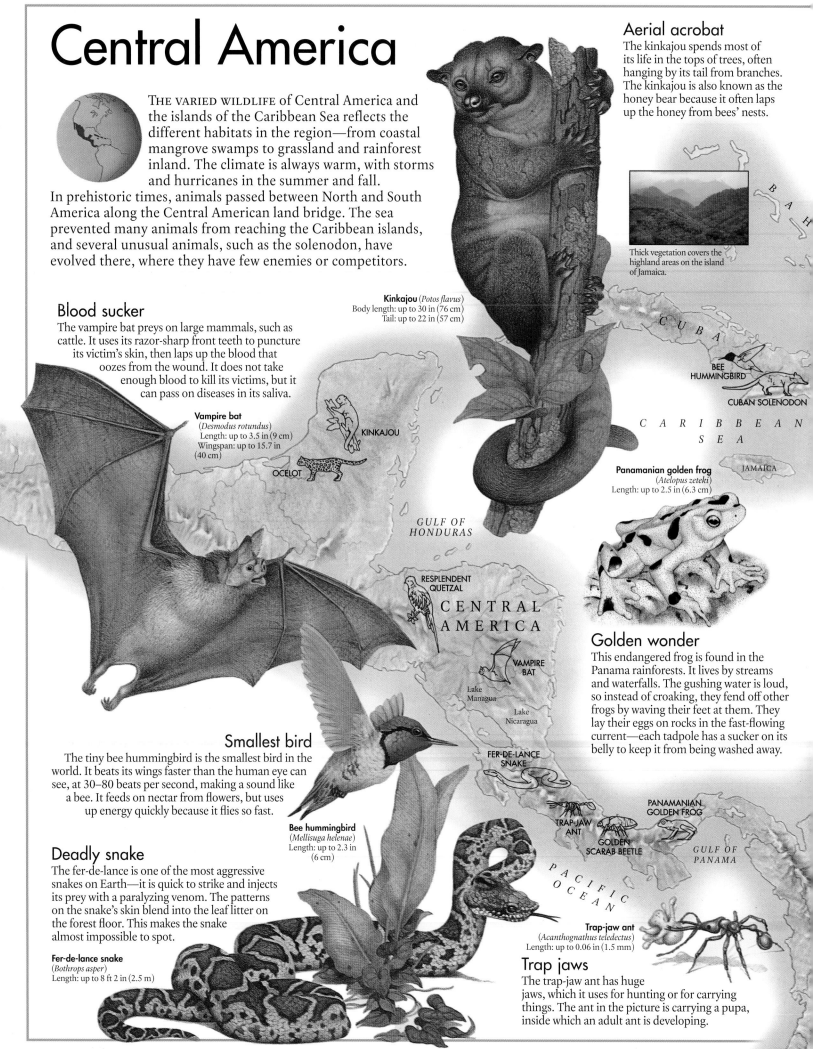

Central America

THE VARIED WILDLIFE of Central America and the islands of the Caribbean Sea reflects the different habitats in the region—from coastal mangrove swamps to grassland and rainforest inland. The climate is always warm, with storms and hurricanes in the summer and fall. In prehistoric times, animals passed between North and South America along the Central American land bridge. The sea prevented many animals from reaching the Caribbean islands, and several unusual animals, such as the solenodon, have evolved there, where they have few enemies or competitors.

Aerial acrobat

The kinkajou spends most of its life in the tops of trees, often hanging by its tail from branches. The kinkajou is also known as the honey bear because it often laps up the honey from bees' nests.

Thick vegetation covers the highland areas on the island of Jamaica.

Kinkajou (*Potos flavus*)
Body length: up to 30 in (76 cm)
Tail: up to 22 in (57 cm)

Blood sucker

The vampire bat preys on large mammals, such as cattle. It uses its razor-sharp front teeth to puncture its victim's skin, then laps up the blood that oozes from the wound. It does not take enough blood to kill its victims, but it can pass on diseases in its saliva.

Vampire bat
(*Desmodus rotundus*)
Length: up to 3.5 in (9 cm)
Wingspan: up to 15.7 in
(40 cm)

KINKAJOU

OCELOT

GULF OF HONDURAS

BAH

CUBA

BEE HUMMINGBIRD

CUBAN SOLENODON

CARIBBEAN SEA

JAMAICA

Golden wonder

This endangered frog is found in the Panama rainforests. It lives by streams and waterfalls. The gushing water is loud, so instead of croaking, they fend off other frogs by waving their feet at them. They lay their eggs on rocks in the fast-flowing current—each tadpole has a sucker on its belly to keep it from being washed away.

Panamanian golden frog
(*Atelopus zeteki*)
Length: up to 2.5 in (6.3 cm)

RESPLENDENT QUETZAL

CENTRAL AMERICA

VAMPIRE BAT

Lake Managua

Lake Nicaragua

FER-DE-LANCE SNAKE

PANAMANIAN GOLDEN FROG

TRAP-JAW ANT

GOLDEN SCARAB BEETLE

GULF OF PANAMA

PACIFIC OCEAN

Smallest bird

The tiny bee hummingbird is the smallest bird in the world. It beats its wings faster than the human eye can see, at 30–80 beats per second, making a sound like a bee. It feeds on nectar from flowers, but uses up energy quickly because it flies so fast.

Bee hummingbird
(*Mellisuga helenae*)
Length: up to 2.3 in
(6 cm)

Deadly snake

The fer-de-lance is one of the most aggressive snakes on Earth—it is quick to strike and injects its prey with a paralyzing venom. The patterns on the snake's skin blend into the leaf litter on the forest floor. This makes the snake almost impossible to spot.

Fer-de-lance snake
(*Bothrops asper*)
Length: up to 8 ft 2 in (2.5 m)

Trap-jaw ant
(*Acanthognathus teledectus*)
Length: up to 0.06 in (1.5 mm)

Trap jaws

The trap-jaw ant has huge jaws, which it uses for hunting or for carrying things. The ant in the picture is carrying a pupa, inside which an adult ant is developing.

Spotted cat

The beautiful ocelot is rarely seen, but each cat has a different pattern of markings on its coat. The ocelot is an excellent climber and swimmer. It comes out at night to hunt for birds, snakes, and small mammals.

Rare animal

A relative of the hedgehog, the Cuban solenodon is a rare animal found only in Cuba. It is in danger of becoming extinct because it reproduces slowly, and is also threatened by new species, such as the mongoose, brought to Cuba by humans.

Ocelot
(*Leopardus pardalis*)
Body length: up to
3 ft 3 in (1 m)
Tail: up to 16 in (41 cm)

Cuban solenodon (*Atopogale cubana*)
Body length: up to 14 in (36 cm)
Tail: up to 7.5 in (19 cm)

Sacred bird

The ancient peoples of Central America once worshipped the brilliantly colored quetzal as the god of the air. They used the male bird's long tail feathers in religious ceremonies. The male sheds his tail feathers after each breeding season and grows new ones the following year.

Resplendent quetzal
(*Pharomachrus mocinno*)
Body length: up to
41 in (105 cm)
Tail: up to 2 ft (60 cm)

HISPANIOLA   PUERTO RICO

Loudest animal

Male howler monkeys are the noisiest land animals in the world. They shout and roar at rival monkeys to tell them to keep out of their territory. The howler has a large voice box that enables it to roar so loudly, it can be heard up to 2 miles (3 km) away.

Ursine red howler
(*Alouatta arctoidea*)
Body length: up to
2 ft 2 in (65 cm)
Tail: up to 2 ft
3 in (68 cm)

Golden scarab beetle (*Chrysina resplendens*)
Length: up to
1.4 in (3.6 cm)

GUADELOUPE

Shiny wings

The metallic sheen on the wing cases of the golden beetle acts as a form of camouflage. The cases reflect the light and make the beetle's outline harder to see.

MARTINIQUE

BARBADOS

ST. VINCENT
AMAZON

SCARLET IBIS

TRINIDAD

Many of the islands were formed by underwater volcanoes. There are still active volcanoes in the region.

URSINE RED
HOWLER

St. Vincent Amazon
(*Amazona guildingii*)
Length: up to
18 in (46 cm)
Wingspan: 2 ft (63 cm)

Handy feet

This parrot lives only on the Caribbean island of St. Vincent. It has unusual feet, with two toes pointing forward and two pointing backward. This gives it a powerful grip on branches and allows it to use its feet like hands. Each parrot is either right- or left-footed.

Scarlet ibis
(*Eudocimus ruber*)
Length: up to 2 ft 4 in (71 cm)
Wingspan: up to 3 ft 5 in (1.05 m)

Curved bill

The scarlet ibis has a long, curved bill, which it uses to probe in soft mud for insects, frogs, crustaceans, and fish. Ibises feed and nest in flocks. They often nest in trees or in areas surrounded by water, where they are safer from enemies. The island of Trinidad is famous for its nesting colonies.

SOUTH AMERICA

Many of the Caribbean islands have beautiful sandy beaches and are popular vacation resorts.

KILOMETERS
0   100   200   300

0   100   200
MILES

19

The Galápagos

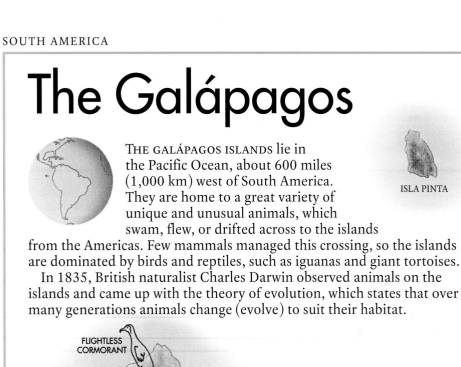

THE GALÁPAGOS ISLANDS lie in the Pacific Ocean, about 600 miles (1,000 km) west of South America. They are home to a great variety of unique and unusual animals, which swam, flew, or drifted across to the islands from the Americas. Few mammals managed this crossing, so the islands are dominated by birds and reptiles, such as iguanas and giant tortoises.

In 1835, British naturalist Charles Darwin observed animals on the islands and came up with the theory of evolution, which states that over many generations animals change (evolve) to suit their habitat.

Useless wings

The ancestor of the flightless cormorant flew to the Galápagos, but today its wings are only one-third of the size they would have to be to support it in flight. Before humans settled on the islands, cormorants had no enemies there it needed to fly away from. Its feathers are also not waterproof, so after diving underwater to catch fish, it spreads out its wings to dry in the sun.

Flightless cormorant
(*Phalacrocorax harrisi*)
Length: up to 3 ft 3 in (1 m)

ISLA PINTA

ISLA GENOVESA

ISLA MARCHENA

FLIGHTLESS CORMORANT

Wolf Volcano

Underwater volcanoes formed the Galápagos Islands, which are made of volcanic lava.

Darwin Volcano

GALÁPAGOS PENGUIN

The smaller Galápagos Islands are largely waterless and few plants can survive.

ISLA FERNANDINA

La Cumbre Volcano

LAND IGUANA

SALLY LIGHTFOOT CRAB

ISLA SAN SALVADOR

Alcedo Volcano

The prickly pear is one of the few plants that can grow on the lava fields.

P A C I F I C
O C E A N

GALÁPAGOS FUR SEAL

ISLA SANTA CRUZ

WOODPECKER FINCH

LITTLE VERMILION FLYCATCHER

I S L A

GIANT TORTOISE

ISLA SANTA FÉ

Santo Tomás Volcano

I S A B E L A

Land iguana
(*Conolophus subcristatus*)
Length: up to 3 ft 11 in (1.2 m)

MARINE IGUANA

KILOMETERS
0 5 10 15 20

0 5 10 15
MILES

Fighting males

During the mating season, the male land iguana defends his territory against other males. If a rival approaches, he bobs his head in a ritual display to warn the intruder to keep away. If this does not work, a fight may break out, with the iguanas trying to bite each other with their strong teeth. They rarely fight to the death, though, and the weaker male usually retreats when he realizes he cannot win.

Fearless footwork

Large numbers of Sally Lightfoot crabs live on the rocky shores of the Galápagos. The crab has a hard shell for protection. As it grows, it sheds its shell from time to time and grows a larger one. The crab runs sideways because its legs are jointed from the side of its body. Its front legs have developed into a pair of pincers for grasping food.

Sally Lightfoot crab
(*Grapsus grapsus*)
Width of shell: up to 3 in (8 cm)

ISLA SANTA MARÍA

Sea lizard

The marine iguana is the only lizard in the world that swims and feeds in the sea. It has a short snout, which enables it to gnaw seaweed off underwater rocks. Its strong claws help it grip the slippery rocks.

Marine iguana
(*Amblyrhynchus cristatus*)
Length: up to 4 ft 3 in (1.3 m)

Trusty tools

Unusually, the woodpecker finch uses a tool to help it find food. This bird feeds on insect grubs, which live under the bark or inside the trunks of trees. It uses a small twig or cactus spine to dig them out. The woodpecker finch may even make the tool itself by breaking a twig to the right length.

Woodpecker finch
(*Geospiza pallida*)
Length: up to 6 in (15 cm)

Pirate of the air

The frigate bird is named after a ship that was often used by pirates. When it sees another bird carrying food, the frigate bird flies after it and forces it to drop the food. Then it swoops down and grabs the stolen food in mid-air. During courtship, the male puffs out his red throat pouch to attract a female.

Magnificent frigate bird
(*Fregata magnificens*)
Length: up to 3 ft 8 in (1.1 m). Wingspan: up to 8 ft (2.4 m)

Blue-footed booby
(*Sula nebouxii*)
Length: up to 3 ft 9 in (84 cm)
Wingspan: up to 5 ft 5 in (1.7 m)

Blue shoes

The blue-footed booby lifts its feet up and down in a comical courtship dance. The name "booby" comes from the Spanish word *bobo*, meaning "clown." The booby feeds on fish, which it catches underwater in its long bill, often plunging into the sea from great heights.

Fur coats

The Galápagos fur seal has a thick coat, which consists of an outer layer of long guard hairs and an inner layer of soft underfur. These seals were hunted almost to extinction for their skins and are still an endangered species today.

Galápagos fur seal
(*Arctocephalus galapagoensis*)
Length: up to 5 ft 3 in (1.6 m)

MAGNIFICENT
FRIGATE BIRD

ISLA SAN CRISTÓBAL

Unique penguin

The Galápagos penguin is the only penguin found on the Equator. It can survive in the Galápagos because of a water current that sweeps past the islands, carrying cold water from the Antarctic.

Galápagos penguin
(*Spheniscus mendiculus*)
Height: up to 21 in (53 cm)

Fly catcher

The little vermilion flycatcher often perches on the back of a giant tortoise so that it can snap up flies disturbed by the tortoise's feet. The male bird has bright red feathers, which he shows off by flying overhead in a display to attract a mate.

Little vermilion flycatcher
(*Pyrocephalus nanus*)
Length: up to 5.5 in (14 cm)

Super shells

The Galápagos are home to several different species of giant tortoises, which live on different islands. Each species has developed a slightly differently shaped shell to suit its habitat and diet. Giant tortoises have survived on the islands because they can go for long periods without food or water and can move easily over rough ground. The name "Galápagos" comes from a Spanish word for tortoise.

BLUE-FOOTED
BOOBY

ISLA ESPAÑOLA

Giant tortoise
(*Chelonoidis nigra*)
Total length: 6 ft 1 in (1.9 m)

The Andes

THE ANDES are the longest chain of mountains in the world. They stretch right down the western side of South America, from the Caribbean Sea in the north to Cape Horn in the south. Below the peaks of the Andes lie high plateaus, studded with lakes. To the east, the land slopes down toward the grasslands of the pampas and the rainforests of the Amazon basin.

Animals that live in the mountains have to cope with the thin air at high altitudes. Some have developed extra-large hearts and lungs to help them get enough oxygen. The temperature in the high Andes drops to around 14°F (–10°C) at night, so animals such as the vicuna have thick coats to keep them warm.

Wide wings

The Andean condor is one of the largest flying birds that has ever lived. It has huge wings and can soar and glide for long distances. The condor eats the flesh of dead animals. Its head and neck are bald, so it can reach into a carcass without dirtying any feathers.

Andean condor
(*Vultur gryphus*)
Wingspan: up to
10 ft 6 in (3.2 m)

Whistling guard

Most vicunas live in a small family group, which is fiercely guarded by an adult male. If the male spots any sign of danger, he whistles loudly to give the alarm so that the females and young can escape. Vicunas can run at speeds of up to 29 mph (47 kph) over long distances.

Digging bird

The dark-faced ground tyrant digs a long underground burrow with a nesting chamber at the end. The bird uses its beak as a pickax and clears away soil with its sharp claws. The ground tyrant runs quickly along the mountain slopes on its long legs, snatching insects from the ground.

Southern pudu
(*Pudu puda*)
Body length:
up to 2 ft 7 in
(80 cm)

Dark-faced ground tyrant
(*Muscisaxicola macloviana*)
Length: up to 6.5 in (16.5 cm)

Smallest deer

At only 15 in (40 cm) tall, the southern pudu is the smallest deer on the American continent. It lives in remote areas of the mountain lowlands and is very shy. This makes it hard to observe, and very little is known about its behavior. It is mostly solitary and feeds on leaves, shoots, and fruit.

Vicuna
(*Vicugna vicugna*)
Height at shoulder: up to 2 ft 11 in (90 cm)
Body length: up to 6 ft 3 in (1.9 m)

Darwin's frog
(*Rhinoderma darwinii*)
Length: up to 0.1 in (0.3 cm)

Frogs in the throat

The male Darwin's frog carries his tadpoles in pouches in his throat to keep them safe from enemies. While the tadpoles are in his throat, the frog can make only a faint call. After 50 to 70 days, the tadpoles change into tiny froglets and the male spits them out. The female plays no part in rearing the young.

Handy nose

The mountain tapir lives in the mountain forests. Its snout and upper lip are joined together to form a short trunk, which it uses as a nose and as an extra hand to tear leaves from branches. Tapirs are hunted by many animals, including the jaguar, and must always be on the lookout for danger.

Mountain tapir
(*Tapirus pinchaque*)
Body length: up to 6 ft 6 in (2 m)

Biggest hummingbird

The Andean giant hummingbird is the largest hummingbird in the world. During the cold nights, its body temperature falls to just above freezing point. This helps the bird save energy, which it would otherwise use to keep its body warm.

Giant hummingbird
(*Patagona gigas*)
Length: up to 8.6 in
(22 cm)

Chiseling beak

The Andean flicker is a type of woodpecker. It uses its strong beak to chisel out a nesting hole in the spiny leaves of a Puya plant. Its feet are adapted for climbing, with two toes pointing forward and two backward.

Andean flicker
(*Colaptes rupicola*)
Length: up to 12.6 in
(32 cm)

Furry coat

Chinchillas live high up in the Andes and have soft, thick fur coats to keep out the cold. They are now rare animals, as humans have killed many to make coats from their fur. Chinchillas make their homes in holes and cracks among the rocks.

Chilean chinchilla (*Chinchilla lanigera*)
Body length: up to 9.5 in (24 cm)
Tail: up to 6.7 in (17 cm)

Changing spectacles

The white markings around the eyes of the spectacled bear make it look as if it is wearing glasses. These markings vary a lot, and each animal has different-shaped spectacles. At night it sleeps in a tree, where it builds a nest of sticks.

Spectacled bear (*Tremarctos ornatus*)
Height at shoulder: up to 2 ft 7 in (80 cm)
Body length: 6 ft 2 in (up to 1.9 m)

Shaggy camel

The alpaca is a relative of the camel. It has a shaggy coat of fine, soft hair that reaches almost to the ground. People use their woolly coats to make clothes. An alpaca's fleece weighs about 6.5 lbs (3 kg).

Alpaca (*Vicugna pacos*)
Height at shoulder: up to 3 ft (90 cm)

Waterfall duck

The torrent duck feeds in the fast-flowing streams and waterfalls of the Andes. It uses its sharp claws to grip slippery boulders and steers through the water with its stiff tail. Its streamlined body shape helps it swim underwater when it dives to look for food.

Torrent duck
(*Merganetta armata*)
Length: up to 18 in (46 cm)

SOUTH AMERICA

MOUNTAIN TAPIR

ANDEAN CONDOR

DARK-FACED GROUND TYRANT

SPECTACLED BEAR

Amazon

A M A Z O N
B A S I N

The Andes range contains 50 peaks that are over 19,700 ft (6,000 m) high.

A variety of birds and animals live in the rushes around Lake Titicaca and feed in the lake itself.

Lake Titicaca

ANDEAN FLICKER

VICUNA

TORRENT DUCK

ALPACA

CHILEAN CHINCHILLA

GIANT HUMMINGBIRD

Salado

Paraná

P A M P A S

SOUTHERN PUDU

Colorado

DARWIN'S FROG

Parinacota is one of the many active volcanoes in the Andes.

A T L A N T I C
O C E A N

FALKLAND ISLANDS

TIERRA DEL FUEGO

CAPE HORN

KILOMETERS
0   200   400   600

0   200   400
MILES

P A C I F I C   O C E A N

PATAGONIA

Amazon Rainforest

THE VAST AMAZON JUNGLE is the largest area of tropical rainforest in the world. It covers about 2,702,700 sq miles (7,000,000 sq km) —an area 12 times the size of France. The rainforest is situated in the huge basin of the Amazon River, which flows 4,000 miles (6,450 km) across South America. The weather in the Amazon basin is hot and humid year round.

The Amazon rainforest is home to a greater variety of wildlife than anywhere else on Earth. Many animals live in the treetops, where there are plenty of leaves, flowers, and fruit to feed on. Some, such as the spider monkey, have grasping tails and long nails to help them swing through the branches. Rainforest birds have short, broad wings and can fly through the trees. On the forest floor, many animals find food with long noses and sharp claws. Today, animals are threatened as humans clear rainforest land to farm and mine.

Reflecting wings
The male morpho butterfly is brilliantly colored because of the way the tiny scales on its wings reflect the light. As the butterfly moves its wings, the colors change. Many morphos have been collected for jewelry or decoration, and they are in danger of becoming extinct.

Rhetenor blue morpho
(*Morpho rhetenor*)
Wingspan: up to 6.7 in (17 cm)

Big bill
With its long, hollow bill, the red-billed toucan can reach fruit on twigs too thin to bear its weight. The jagged edges of the bill work like a saw to cut fruit, which the toucan tosses back into its throat. The bright colors help the bird recognize others of its kind.

Red-billed toucan
(*Ramphastos tucanus*)
Length: up to 1 ft 10 in (58 cm)

Underwater danger
The caiman is a type of crocodile. It lurks underwater with just its nose and eyes showing above the water. When a thirsty animal comes for a drink, the caiman snaps it up with its sharp teeth and holds it underwater until it drowns.

Spectacled caiman
(*Caiman crocodilus*)
Body length: up to 7 ft 11 in (2.4 m)

Hoatzin
(*Opisthocomus hoazin*)
Length: up to 2 ft 3 in (70 cm)

Weak wings
The hoatzin has such weak flight muscles that it cannot fly more than 330 ft (100 m) or so before it has to crash-land for a rest. It uses its wings and tail for extra support as it climbs through the trees. Young hoatzins have little claws on their wings to help them climb.

Acrobatic leaps
The spider monkey is an amazing acrobat. It makes leaps of 33 ft (10 m) or more through the trees, using its tail like a hand or foot. This type of tail is called prehensile. Underneath its tail is a patch of ridged skin, which helps it get a firm grip on the branches.

Black spider monkey
(*Ateles chamek*)
Body length: up to 2 ft (60 cm)
Tail: up to 2 ft 10 in (88 cm)

Jaguar (*Panthera onca*)
Height to shoulder: up to 2 ft 7 in (80 cm)
Body length: up to 5 ft 9 in (1.7 m)

Spotted cat
The jaguar is the largest cat in South America. Unlike the leopard, it has black marks inside each ring of spots. Its coat acts as a camouflage in the forest, and it can creep up on the animals it hunts without being seen.

CARIBBEAN

Lake Maracaibo

GULF OF PANAMA

The highest parts of the rainforest receive 120 in (305 cm) of rain each year.

HARPY EAGLE

Amazon

BROWN-THROATED THREE-TOED SLOTH

PACIFIC OCEAN

ANDES MTS

A M

SCARLET MACAW

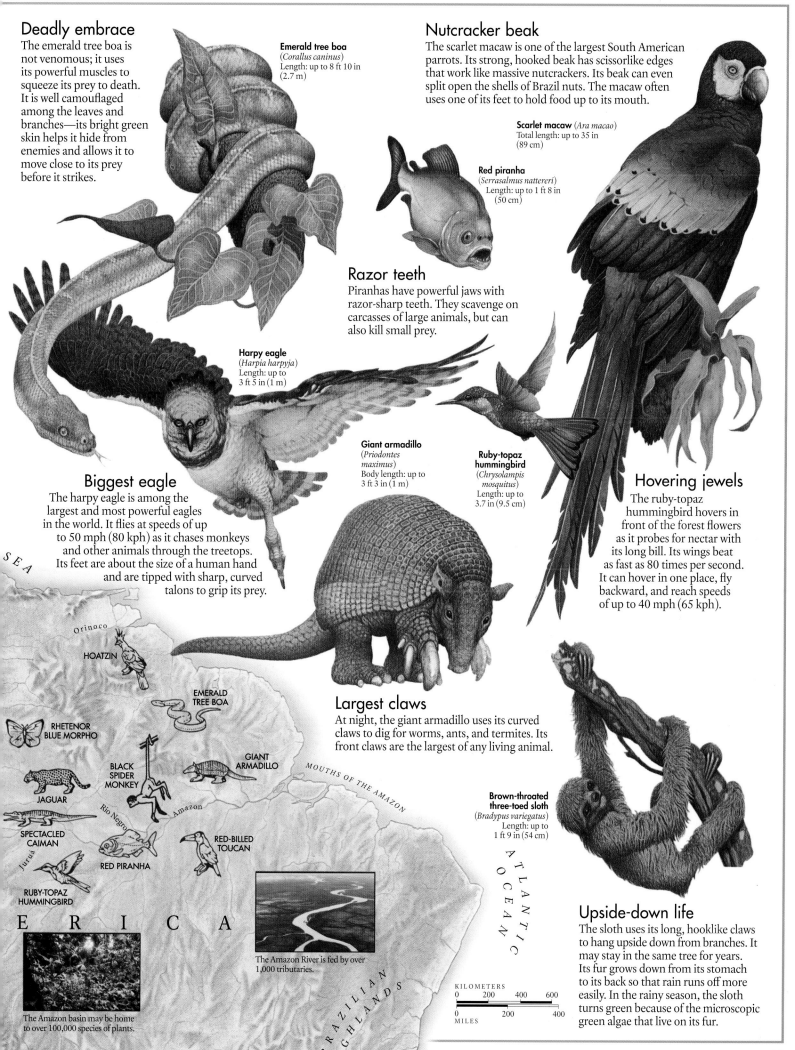

Deadly embrace

The emerald tree boa is not venomous; it uses its powerful muscles to squeeze its prey to death. It is well camouflaged among the leaves and branches—its bright green skin helps it hide from enemies and allows it to move close to its prey before it strikes.

Emerald tree boa
(*Corallus caninus*)
Length: up to 8 ft 10 in
(2.7 m)

Nutcracker beak

The scarlet macaw is one of the largest South American parrots. Its strong, hooked beak has scissorlike edges that work like massive nutcrackers. Its beak can even split open the shells of Brazil nuts. The macaw often uses one of its feet to hold food up to its mouth.

Scarlet macaw (*Ara macao*)
Total length: up to 35 in
(89 cm)

Red piranha
(*Serrasalmus nattereri*)
Length: up to 1 ft 8 in
(50 cm)

Razor teeth

Piranhas have powerful jaws with razor-sharp teeth. They scavenge on carcasses of large animals, but can also kill small prey.

Harpy eagle
(*Harpia harpyja*)
Length: up to
3 ft 5 in (1 m)

Biggest eagle

The harpy eagle is among the largest and most powerful eagles in the world. It flies at speeds of up to 50 mph (80 kph) as it chases monkeys and other animals through the treetops. Its feet are about the size of a human hand and are tipped with sharp, curved talons to grip its prey.

Giant armadillo
(*Priodontes maximus*)
Body length: up to
3 ft 3 in (1 m)

Ruby-topaz hummingbird
(*Chrysolampis mosquitus*)
Length: up to
3.7 (9.5 cm)

Hovering jewels

The ruby-topaz hummingbird hovers in front of the forest flowers as it probes for nectar with its long bill. Its wings beat as fast as 80 times per second. It can hover in one place, fly backward, and reach speeds of up to 40 mph (65 kph).

Largest claws

At night, the giant armadillo uses its curved claws to dig for worms, ants, and termites. Its front claws are the largest of any living animal.

Brown-throated three-toed sloth
(*Bradypus variegatus*)
Length: up to
1 ft 9 in (54 cm)

Upside-down life

The sloth uses its long, hooklike claws to hang upside down from branches. It may stay in the same tree for years. Its fur grows down from its stomach to its back so that rain runs off more easily. In the rainy season, the sloth turns green because of the microscopic green algae that live on its fur.

SEA

Orinoco

HOATZIN

EMERALD
TREE BOA

RHETENOR
BLUE MORPHO

BLACK
SPIDER
MONKEY

GIANT
ARMADILLO

JAGUAR

Rio Negro

Amazon

SPECTACLED
CAIMAN

Juruá

RED-BILLED
TOUCAN

RED PIRANHA

RUBY-TOPAZ
HUMMINGBIRD

MOUTHS OF THE AMAZON

E R I C A

The Amazon basin may be home
to over 100,000 species of plants.

The Amazon River is fed by over
1,000 tributaries.

ATLANTIC OCEAN

BRAZILIAN HIGHLANDS

KILOMETERS
0   200   400   600

0   200   400
MILES

Lake Tiricaca

The Pampas

THE PAMPAS IS A VAST GRASSY plain that covers an area of almost 300,000 sq miles (777,000 sq km) in South America. The climate in the pampas is generally dry. Although grasses flourish in these conditions, trees and larger plants can survive only along river banks. Termite mounds, which can be up to 6 ft 6 in (2 m) high, dot the pampas plain.

Many pampas animals, such as the armadillo, live in underground burrows. This protects them from fires, which are common on the dry grassland. Much of the pampas is now used by farmers for grazing cattle. Wild animals face extra competition for food, and some species are declining as a result.

Speedy sprinter

The rhea is a flightless bird. It can run at speeds of more than 30 mph (50 kph). The male rhea rears the chicks and defends the nest. He will attack anything that comes too close, even people or small airplanes.

Greater rhea
(*Rhea americana*)
Height: up to
4 ft 7 in (1.4 m)

Long jump

The mara, or Patagonian hare, has long back legs, which it uses to bound away from danger. It can cover up to 6 ft 6 in (2 m) in one leap. Although the mara looks like a hare, it is in fact related to the guinea pig. Maras live in pairs, but sometimes use communal burrows for breeding.

Patagonian mara (*Dolichotis patagonum*)
Body length: up to 2 ft 7 in (80 cm)

Ovenbird

The rufous hornero is a kind of ovenbird—so named because their nests look like earthenware ovens. The female bird builds the nest from up to 2,500 lumps of mud. The nest is often built on a post because there are few trees on the pampas.

Rufous hornero
(*Furnarius rufus*)
Length: up to
9 in (23 cm)

Pink fairy armadillo
(*Chlamyphorus truncatus*)
Body length: up to 6 in (15 cm)

Chain mail

The pink fairy armadillo has protective armor on its back, made of plates of bone covered with horny scales. It uses the huge claws on its front feet for digging. Because it spends a lot of time underground, its eyes are tiny and its sight is poor.

Rare deer

The pampas deer is one of the few large plant-eating animals left on the grasslands, but its existence is threatened by farmers and hunters. The male has glands on his hooves that give off a smell, which can be detected more than 1 mile (1.5 km) away.

Bullying bird

The southern caracara is a bird of prey. It eats insects and other small animals, but it also likes carrion (the flesh of dead animals). The caracara sometimes pecks and bullies a vulture until it forces it to cough up some of the carrion it has just eaten.

Plains viscacha
(*Lagostomus maximus*)
Body length: up to 2 ft (61.5 cm)
Tail: up to 8 in (20 cm)

Southern caracara (*Polyborus plancus*)
Length: up to 2 ft 1 in (64 cm)

Underground city

Viscachas are rodents that dig huge networks of tunnels under the pampas. Many generations of viscachas may live in the same burrow. The viscacha digs mainly with its front feet, pushing soil out of the way with its nose. It closes its nostrils to keep soil from getting in.

Pampas deer
(*Odocoileus bezoarticus*)
Height at shoulder:
2 ft 3 in (70 cm)

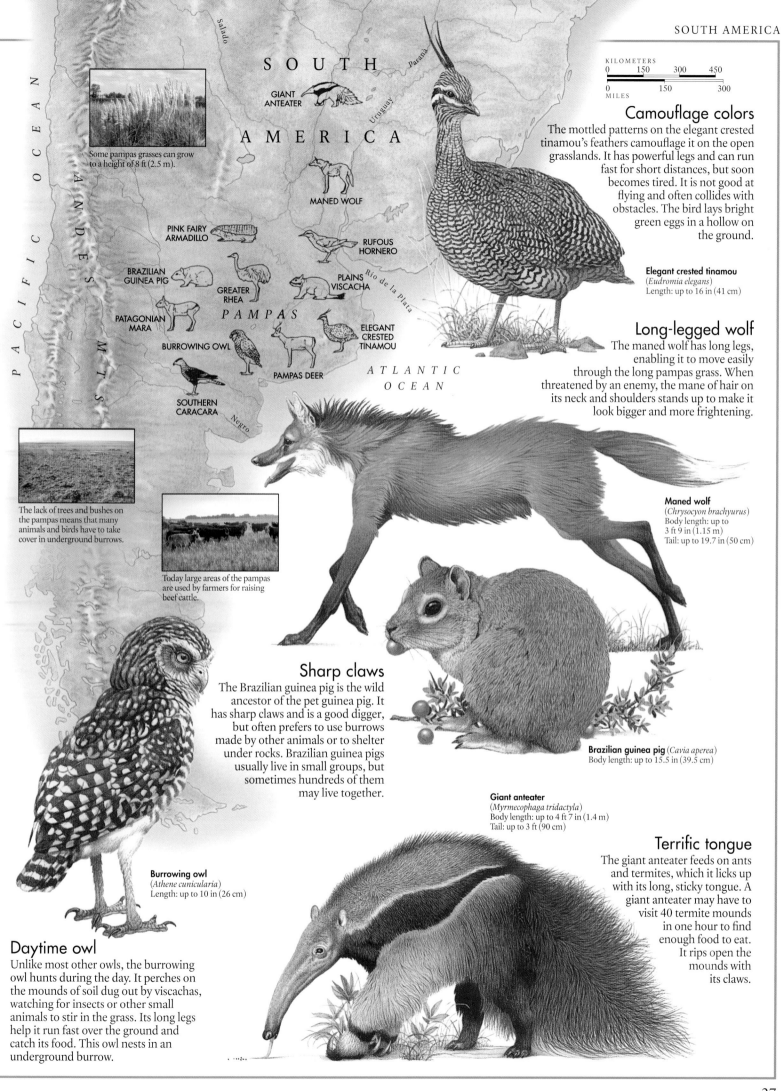

SOUTH AMERICA

Salado

GIANT ANTEATER

Uruguay

Paraná

MANED WOLF

PINK FAIRY ARMADILLO

BRAZILIAN GUINEA PIG

GREATER RHEA

PATAGONIAN MARA

BURROWING OWL

SOUTHERN CARACARA

PAMPAS

PAMPAS DEER

RUFOUS HORNERO

PLAINS VISCACHA

Río de la Plata

ELEGANT CRESTED TINAMOU

ATLANTIC OCEAN

Negro

PACIFIC OCEAN

ANDES MTS

Some pampas grasses can grow to a height of 8 ft (2.5 m).

The lack of trees and bushes on the pampas means that many animals and birds have to take cover in underground burrows.

Today large areas of the pampas are used by farmers for raising beef cattle.

Camouflage colors

The mottled patterns on the elegant crested tinamou's feathers camouflage it on the open grasslands. It has powerful legs and can run fast for short distances, but soon becomes tired. It is not good at flying and often collides with obstacles. The bird lays bright green eggs in a hollow on the ground.

Elegant crested tinamou
(*Eudromia elegans*)
Length: up to 16 in (41 cm)

Long-legged wolf

The maned wolf has long legs, enabling it to move easily through the long pampas grass. When threatened by an enemy, the mane of hair on its neck and shoulders stands up to make it look bigger and more frightening.

Maned wolf
(*Chrysocyon brachyurus*)
Body length: up to 3 ft 9 in (1.15 m)
Tail: up to 19.7 in (50 cm)

Sharp claws

The Brazilian guinea pig is the wild ancestor of the pet guinea pig. It has sharp claws and is a good digger, but often prefers to use burrows made by other animals or to shelter under rocks. Brazilian guinea pigs usually live in small groups, but sometimes hundreds of them may live together.

Brazilian guinea pig (*Cavia aperea*)
Body length: up to 15.5 in (39.5 cm)

Giant anteater
(*Myrmecophaga tridactyla*)
Body length: up to 4 ft 7 in (1.4 m)
Tail: up to 3 ft (90 cm)

Terrific tongue

The giant anteater feeds on ants and termites, which it licks up with its long, sticky tongue. A giant anteater may have to visit 40 termite mounds in one hour to find enough food to eat. It rips open the mounds with its claws.

Burrowing owl
(*Athene cunicularia*)
Length: up to 10 in (26 cm)

Daytime owl

Unlike most other owls, the burrowing owl hunts during the day. It perches on the mounds of soil dug out by viscachas, watching for insects or other small animals to stir in the grass. Its long legs help it run fast over the ground and catch its food. This owl nests in an underground burrow.

Conifer Forests

A THICK BAND OF DENSE EVERGREEN FOREST stretches across the northern parts of Europe, covering large areas of Scotland and Scandinavia. There are smaller evergreen forests farther south, such as the Black Forest in Germany and the Ardennes in Belgium. The most common trees in these forests are conifers (trees that have cones), such as pines, spruces, and firs. In recent years, acid rain, which is especially harmful to trees with needlelike leaves, has damaged many European conifer forests.

Animals that live in these forests have to survive in a severe climate. The winters are bitterly cold, but most conifer trees keep their leaves year round and provide some shelter. Some forest animals, such as the stoat, grow white coats in the winter so that they are camouflaged against the snow. Other animals, such as the wood ant, hibernate during the winter, while some birds, such as the osprey, migrate south to warmer places.

Fish snatcher

The osprey feeds on fish that it snatches from lakes. It has long, sharp claws and horny spines under its toes, which enable it to grip a slippery fish. An adult osprey can carry a fish weighing up to 4.5 lbs (2 kg). In the fall, the osprey migrates to Africa, where the weather is warmer and there are plenty of fish for it to eat.

Osprey (*Pandion haliaetus*)
Length: up to 2 ft 1 in (64 cm)
Wingspan: up to 5 ft 9 in (1.7 m)

Northern long-eared owl (*Asio otus*)
Length: up to 16 in (40 cm)
Wingspan: up to 3 ft 3 in (1 m)

Long ears

The brown long-eared bat's huge ears are three-quarters the length of its body. They are so big that a young bat cannot hold its ears up straight until it is old enough to fly. The bat feeds on moths, midges, and flies. During the cold winter months, it hibernates in a cave.

Brown long-eared bat
(*Plecotus auritus*)
Wingspan: up to 11 in (28 cm)

Underground city

Wood ants build huge nests on the forest floor from pine needles and other plant material. Nests keep the ants warm in winter, when they hibernate in the soil beneath the mound. When threatened, a wood ant sprays its enemy with a stinging liquid called formic acid from glands on its abdomen.

Wood ant (*Formica rufa*) Length: up to 0.35 in (0.9 cm)

False ears

The "ears" of the northern long-eared owl are only tufts of feathers—its ear openings are on the sides of its head. It hunts at night using its sharp eyesight and good hearing to find small mammals on the floor.

Wild cat (*Felis silvestris*)
Body length: up to 2 ft 5 in (74 cm)
Tail: up to 14.5 in (37 cm)

Red crossbill
(*Loxia curvirostra*)
Length: up to 7.8 in (20 cm)

Crossed beak

The crossbill uses its crossed beak to tear open pine cones, so it can lick out the seeds. Adult crossbills regurgitate partly digested seeds to feed their young. Every few years, crossbills move out of their normal breeding areas and invade other parts of Europe. If conditions are good, they may settle in the new area for one or more seasons.

Stripey tail

The wild cat is closely related to the domestic cat, but it is slightly bigger and has a thicker tail with black rings on it. The wild cat hunts at night for small mammals, birds, and insects. The forests provide it with cover for hunting.

Eaten alive

The female giant ichneumon lays her eggs next to the larvae of wood wasps, which the young grubs feed on when they hatch. Because wasp larvae tunnel deep inside tree trunks, the ichneumon drills through the wood with an egg-laying tube, which is 1.5 in (4 cm) long.

Giant ichneumon (*Rhyssa persuasoria*)
Length: up to 1.6 in (4 cm)

Antler fights

In the fall mating season, called the rut, the male red deer fights rival males with his antlers to win females for mating. He sheds his antlers each spring. New ones grow in time for the next mating season.

Western capercaillie (*Tetrao urogallus*)
Length: up to 3 ft 9 in (1.15 m)

Western red deer (*Cervus elaphus*)
Height at shoulder: up to 4 ft 3 in (1.3 m)
Body length: up to 8 ft 9 in (2 m)

Flying acrobat

The pine marten is an acrobatic and swift nighttime hunter. It has strong legs, broad pads, and long claws that help it climb, and its bushy tail helps it balance. It eats many things, from small birds to rats, beetles, and fruit. It hunts on the ground and in the trees.

Dancing display

In spring, the male capercaillie puts on a display to attract females. He fans out his tail, points his neck upward, and makes odd gurgling sounds. He may even jump and clap his wings. Displaying capercaillies are very aggressive and will threaten deer, sheep, or even humans who disturb them.

European pine marten (*Martes martes*)
Body length: up to 23 in (58 cm)

Smelly protection

If it is threatened, the polecat produces a foul-smelling liquid from glands under its tail. The polecat also uses this scent to mark its territory. Polecats do not hibernate, and hunt for small mammals all year round.

Polecat (*Mustela putorius*)
Body: up to 18 in (46 cm)

Winters in the forests are bitterly cold, with snow covering the ground for up to half the year.

EUROPEAN PINE MARTEN

OSPREY

RED CROSSBILL

Lake Onega

Lake Ladoga

WILD CAT

N O R T H S E A

WESTERN CAPERCAILLIE

WOOD ANT

NORTHERN LONG-EARED OWL

B R I T I S H I S L E S

The many lakes in the northern European forests provide animals with places to drink.

GIANT ICHNEUMON

B A L T I C S E A

BROWN LONG-EARED BAT

POLECAT

Many European conifer forests have been planted by people and are harvested for their timber.

KILOMETERS
0 100 200 300 400

ENGLISH CHANNEL

0 100 200
MILES

N O R T H E R N

Wisła

ARDENNES FOREST

Oder

E U R O P E

WESTERN RED DEER

BLACK FOREST

Danube

29

Woodlands

THE BROADLEAVED WOODLANDS of Europe provide food and shelter for a rich variety of animals. Insects feed on the leaves, birds and mammals nest in the trunks and branches, and creatures such as woodlice and beetles live in the leaf litter on the woodland floor. The weather changes with the seasons, and this affects animal behavior. In the warm spring days, insects emerge, birds begin to nest, and young mammals are born. In the hot summer months, there is plenty of food and young animals grow quickly. In the fall, most of the trees lose their leaves, and the animals feast on fruits and berries or store food for the winter. The long, cold nights and short days make winter difficult for animals. Many grow thick coats and spend more time in their homes. Some birds fly away to spend the winter in warmer climates.

Caterpillar diet

In spring and summer, blue tits feed their young mainly on caterpillars. While the young are in the nest, their parents may bring them more than 10,000 items of food. In winter, blue tits feed in mixed flocks with other small birds.

Eurasian blue tit
(*Cyanistes caeruleus*)
Length: up to 4.7 in (12 cm)

Nutcracker beak

The nuthatch often wedges a nut in the bark of a tree and hammers it open with its beak. It is the only bird that can climb headfirst down trees, searching for insects under the bark as it moves.

Eurasian nuthatch
(*Sitta europaea*)
Length: up to 6.7 in (17 cm)

European badger (*Meles meles*)
Body length: up to 3 ft (90 cm)
Tail: up to 8 in (20 cm)

Strong digger

Badgers have strong front legs and long, sharp claws that they use to dig out extensive underground burrows, called setts. The tunnels can be up to 65 ft (20 m) long. Generations of badgers may live in the same sett for hundreds of years. When digging, badgers can close their ears and nostrils to keep out dirt.

European stag beetle
(*Lucanus cervus*)
Length including antlers:
up to 3 in (7.5 cm)

Antler jaws

The male European stag beetle has huge jaws that look like stags' antlers. He uses them to fight rivals. Females lay eggs in rotting wood, which the larvae feed on until adulthood.

Northern Europe has a warm, wet climate; many rivers flow through the woodlands.

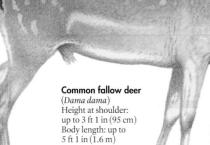

Common fallow deer
(*Dama dama*)
Height at shoulder:
up to 3 ft 1 in (95 cm)
Body length: up to
5 ft 1 in (1.6 m)

Summer spots

In summer, the fallow deer has white spots on its coat, which help camouflage it among the leaves. In winter its coat turns darker. Adult males use their antlers to fight each other over females.

Super snout

The Eurasian wild pig uses its long, sensitive nose to search along the woodland floor for roots, bulbs, nuts, mushrooms, and small creatures. The young have striped coats that make them hard to see and protect them from enemies.

Eurasian wild pig
(*Sus scrofa*)
Height at shoulder:
up to 3 ft 7 in (1.1 m)
Body length: up to
3 ft 3 in (1 m)

BRITISH ISLES
ATLANTIC OCEAN
IRISH SEA
EURASIAN BLUE TIT
EURASIAN NUTHATCH
NO S E
EUROPEAN BADGER
LEAST WEASEL
ENGLISH CHANNEL
E
EUROPEAN STAG BEETLE
GREAT SPOTTED WOODPECKER
Loire
WEST EUROPEAN HEDGEHOG
EURASIAN WILD PIG
PYRENEES
Rhône

Tree acrobat

The red squirrel's long, bushy tail helps it balance as it leaps from tree to tree. It may also flip its tail to warn others of danger. The squirrel has long, strong back legs and hooked claws, which help it grip tree bark.

Eurasian red squirrel
(*Sciurus vulgaris*)
Body length: up to 10 in
(25 cm)
Tail: up to 8 in (20 cm)

West European hedgehog
(*Erinaceus europaeus*)
Length: up to 9.6 in (24.5 cm)

Prickly armor

A hedgehog has 7,000 spines or more on its back. Spines are really modified hairs. Although they are hollow, they are very strong and have sharp points. When a hedgehog is alarmed, it rolls into a ball to protect its underparts with its spines. Baby hedgehogs have soft spines so they do not scratch their mothers while suckling.

Clinging claws

The great spotted woodpecker has curved claws that help it cling to tree bark, and stiff tail feathers to support its weight against the trunk. It uses its long tongue to reach insects in trees' cracks and crevices.

Great spotted woodpecker
(*Dendrocopos major*)
Length: up to 9.5 in (24 cm)

Tawny owl (*Strix aluco*)
Length: up to 1 ft 3 in (39 cm)
Wingspan: up to 3 ft 4 in (1 m)

Silent wings

The tawny owl hunts at night. It has soft, fringed wing feathers that are specially suited for silent flying. It can see well in the dark and has very good hearing. Its prey are small creatures, such as mice and voles, which it seizes with its curved talons.

Hazel dormouse
(*Muscardinus avellanarius*)
Body length: up to 3.5 in (9 cm)
Tail: up to
3.4 in (8.6 cm)

H

E U R O P E

EURASIAN
RED SQUIRREL

Elbe

COMMON
FALLOW DEER

Rhine

RED FOX

HAZEL
DORMOUSE

TAWNY
OWL

KILOMETERS
0   100   200   300

0   100   200
MILES

Rotting leaves litter the woodland floor and provide a rich source of food for plants and insects.

There are many gaps in the trees that let light down to the woodland floor.

Danube

A L P S

Winter sleeper

The dormouse hibernates through the cold winter months in a warm nest of leaves and grass, usually under leaf litter or in a hollow tree stump. The dormouse prepares for hibernation by eating as much as possible in the fall and may nearly double in weight.

Slim hunter

The weasel has a long, thin body, which it squeezes into the burrows of mice and voles to stop them escaping. The weasel is strong for its size and can kill larger animals, such as rabbits.

Least weasel (*Mustela nivalis*)
Body length: up to 10 in (26 cm)
Tail: up to 3.5 in
(9 cm)

Red fox (*Vulpes vulpes*)
Height at shoulder: up to 17.5 in (45 cm)
Body length: up to 3 ft (90 cm)

Night hunter

Red foxes hunt mainly at night. They eat almost anything, from rabbits and earthworms to fish and apples. Although their natural habitat is woodland, many foxes have now adapted to live in towns. They often come out at night to search in people's trash bins for food.

Southern Europe

THE COUNTRIES OF SOUTHERN EUROPE lie around the northern coast of the Mediterranean Sea. They have a climate of long, hot, dry summers with cooler, wetter winters. The typical landscape of this region is dry scrubland. Large numbers of people live in southern Europe or go there on vacation. People have destroyed most of the region's forests and polluted the sea, but there are still some refuges for wildlife, such as the Alps and Pyrenees mountains, the marshlands of the Coto Doñana in Spain, and the Camargue in France. Some rare animals, such as the chamois, live in these protected areas. Southern Europe is also famous for its birdlife. Huge numbers of birds fly across the region on their regular migration routes between Europe and Africa.

Lammergeyer
(*Gypaetus barbatus*)
Length: up to 4 ft 1 in (1.25 m)
Wingspan: up to 9 ft 3 in (2.8 m)

Bone breaker

The lammergeyer, or bearded vulture, feeds on bones that it scavenges from dead animals. Before it starts to feed, it waits until other vultures have pecked all the meat off the bones. The lammergeyer sometimes drops bones from a great height so that they crack open. It can then eat the marrow inside.

Brown bear (*Ursus arctos*)
Height at shoulder: up to 5 ft (1.5 m)
Body length: up to 9 ft 2 in (2.8 m)

Alpine chamois
(*Rupicapra rupicapra*)
Height at shoulder: up to 2 ft 10 in (85 cm)
Body length: up to 4 ft 3 in (1.3 m)

Clinging feet

The nimble Alpine chamois leaps around the rocky crags in mountainous areas of southern Europe. It has strong legs and a spongy pad under each hoof, which helps it grip steep or slippery surfaces. Its leaps can be more than 19 ft (6 m) long and 13 ft (4 m) high.

Blind cave-dweller

The olm, or cave salamander, lives in underground pools and streams. Its eyes are covered in skin because it does not need to see in the dark. It breathes partly through the gills on its head.

Olm
(*Proteus anguinus*)
Length: up to 15.7 in (40 cm)

Name call

The hoopoe is named after its call, which sounds like "hoo-poo-poo." Young hoopoes drive enemies away from their nest by producing a strong smell, hissing loudly, and poking their bills upward.

Nearsighted bear

The brown bear is nearsighted, so it relies on its keen sense of smell to find food. It is mostly vegetarian, using its long claws to dig up roots, shoots, and bulbs. In the fall, the bear fattens up to prepare for its winter hibernation. It lives in the mountains of southern Europe.

Common hoopoe
(*Upupa epops*)
Length: up to 12.6 in (32 cm)

Green toad (*Bufo viridis*)
Length: up to 4.7 in (12 cm)

Insect gobbler

The green toad comes out in the cool, moist night air to hunt for insects. It sometimes enters villages to hunt around street lamps and other sources of light that attract insects. The toad has no teeth and swallows its food whole.

SOUTHERN

EURASIAN GOLDEN ORIOLE

COMMON HOOPOE

ALPS

BAY OF BISCAY

Dordogne
Garonne

GREATER FLAMINGO

LAMMERGEYER

Douro

BROWN BEAR

CORSICA

COMMON GENET

SARDINIA

BALEARIC ISLANDS

MED

IBERIAN LYNX

ROCK OF GIBRALTAR

ATLANTIC OCEAN

BARBARY MACAQUE

The typical Mediterranean habitat consists of dry scrubland covered with thorny shrubs and small trees.

NORTH

Common genet
(*Genetta genetta*)
Body length: up to
1 ft 8 in (52 cm)
Tail: up to
20 in (51 cm)

Spotted stalker

The common genet is nocturnal, coming out at night to stalk small mammals, nesting birds, reptiles, and insects. Its keen eyesight, smell, and hearing make it a good hunter, and its sharp claws help it climb on tree trunks and branches.

Filter beak

The greater flamingo wades through shallow water using its webbed feet to stir up shrimp and other small animals from the bottom. Its beak contains fringes, which filter animals out of the water.

Greater flamingo
(*Phoenicopterus roseus*)
Length: up to 4 ft 9 in (1.45 m)
Wingspan: up to 5 ft 5 in (1.65 m)

Gibraltar monkey

Barbary macaques live on the Rock of Gibraltar. The natural home for this monkey is north Africa, but it is thought that humans brought them to the island from Algeria.

Streamer wings

The male thread-wing ant-lion has long, thin back wings that look like streamers. Large groups of males dance up and down displaying their wings, probably to attract females.

Thread-wing ant-lion
(*Nemoptera sinuata*)
Wingspan: up to 3 in
(8 cm)

Barbary macaque (*Macaca sylvanus*)
Body length: up to 2 ft 1 in (64 cm)

Iberian lynx (*Lynx pardinus*)
Body length: up to 2 ft 8 in (82 cm)
Tail: up to 6 in (16 cm)

Rare cat

The Iberian lynx was once widespread, but its numbers have been drastically reduced by hunting and the destruction of forests. Today it is found only in two parts of southwestern Spain. The lynx lives alone and hunts for small mammals and birds at night.

Eurasian golden oriole
(*Oriolus oriolus*)
Length: up to 9.8 in (25 cm)

Golden bird

The male Eurasian golden oriole has bright yellow and black feathers, which help him attract a female. The female's green feathers provide camouflage when she sits on the nest. In winter, golden orioles migrate to Africa.

EUROPE

ALPINE
CHAMOIS

OLM

The Camargue is a marshy area in southern France, famous for its wild horses, bulls, and flamingos.

THREAD-WING
ANT-LION

GREEN
TOAD

MEDITERRANEAN
MONK SEAL

SICILY

KILOMETERS
0   150   300   450

0   150   300
MILES

The Mediterranean coastline is dotted with beaches where turtles and seals come ashore to breed.

Seal survivor

The Mediterranean monk seal is one of the rarest seals in the world. It once lived all around the Mediterranean Sea, but it was hunted, and the beaches where it used to rest and breed were taken over by vacationers.

CRETE

MEDITERRANEAN SEA

AFRICA

**Mediterranean
monk seal**
(*Monachus
monachus*)
Length: up to
9 ft 2 in (2.8 m)

33

The Sahara

THE SHIFTING SANDS of the Sahara Desert stretch across 3,475,000 sq miles (9,000,000 sq km) of northern Africa, an area almost as big as the United States. The Sahara is the largest desert in the world. In the baking heat of the day, the temperature soars to over 122°F (50°C) in the shade. But at night it is bitterly cold. In some parts of the desert there may be no rain at all for several years.

The animals that live in the Sahara have adapted to this harsh environment in a variety of ways. Many small animals hide in burrows during the day and come out only at dawn and dusk, when it is cooler. Most desert animals can go for long periods without water. Some never drink—they get all the moisture they need from the plants and insects they eat.

Furry feet
The sand cat has thick fur under its feet. This stops it from sinking into the soft sand and protects it from the sand's heat. When it hunts, its large ears enable it to hear and locate animals from a long way off.

Sand cat (*Felis margarita*)
Height at shoulder: up to 13.8 in (35 cm)
Body length: up to 20.4 in (52 cm)

Sandfish
(*Scincus scincus*)
Length including tail:
up to 8 in (20 cm)

Sand swimmer
The sandfish gets its name from the way it "swims" through sand. The lizard's streamlined shape helps it dive into the sand, wriggling from side to side. This behavior helps it avoid the Sun's burning heat.

Prickly hunter
The desert hedgehog spends the day in a burrow and hunts at night. Its long legs lift its body above the hot sand. It often eats scorpions, biting off the stinger first.

Desert hedgehog
(*Paraechinus aethiopicus*)
Length: up to 9.5 in (24 cm)

Desert scorpion
(*Androctonus australis*)
Length: up to 4 in (10 cm)

The Sahara contains several hot, dry, mountainous regions where few plants and animals can survive.

Sand dunes in the Sahara are called "ergs," and can be up to 590 ft (180 m) high.

Super sting
The desert scorpion defends itself with the stinger at the end of its tail. The sting is as venomous as a cobra bite and can kill a much larger animal, such as a dog, in only seven minutes.

Big ears
The fennec fox has huge ears that can be up to 6 in (15 cm) long. The large, thin surface of its ears allows heat to escape from its body and helps keep it cool. When it hunts, the fox can hear its prey moving around.

Fennec fox (*Vulpes zerda*)
Body length: up to 15.5 in (39.5 cm)
Tail: up to 9.8 in (25 cm)

Champion jumper
The jerboa is like a tiny kangaroo. It can jump up to 8 ft (2.5 m) in one bound to escape from enemies. Its strong back legs are four times as long as its front legs. Its long tail helps the jerboa balance when it jumps.

Lesser Egyptian jerboa (*Jaculus jaculus*)
Body length: up to 5 in (13 cm)
Tail: up to 7.7 in (19.7 cm)

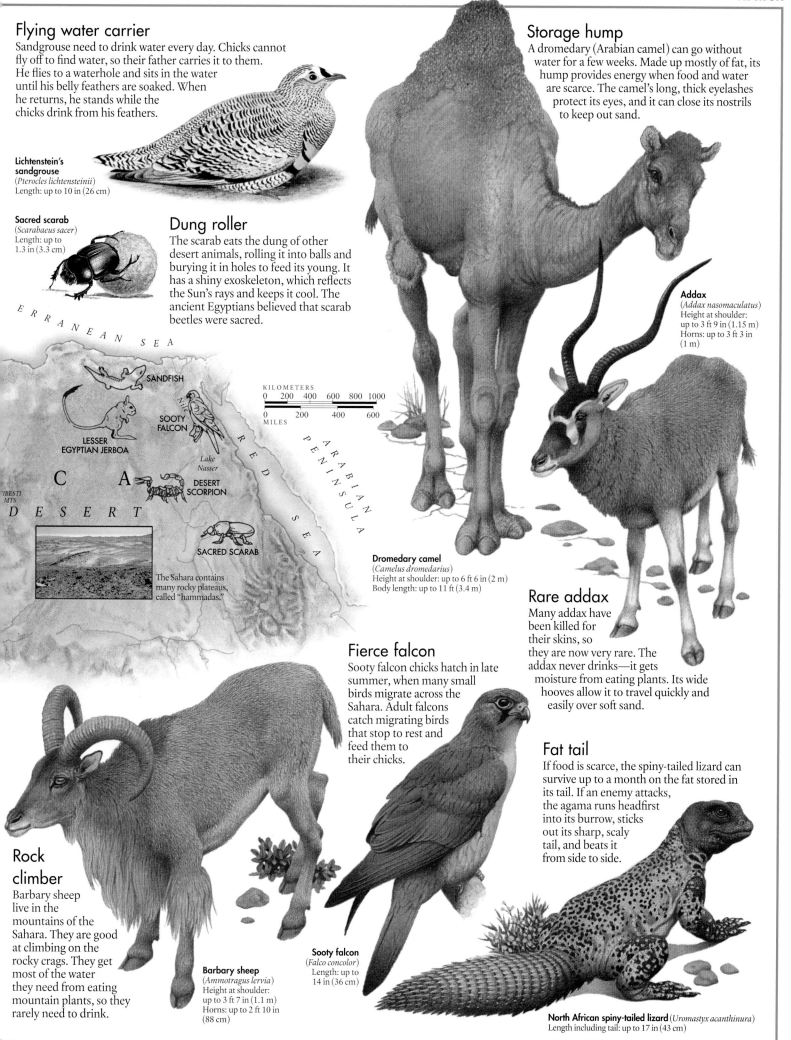

Flying water carrier

Sandgrouse need to drink water every day. Chicks cannot fly off to find water, so their father carries it to them. He flies to a waterhole and sits in the water until his belly feathers are soaked. When he returns, he stands while the chicks drink from his feathers.

Lichtenstein's sandgrouse
(*Pterocles lichtensteinii*)
Length: up to 10 in (26 cm)

Sacred scarab
(*Scarabaeus sacer*)
Length: up to 1.3 in (3.3 cm)

Dung roller

The scarab eats the dung of other desert animals, rolling it into balls and burying it in holes to feed its young. It has a shiny exoskeleton, which reflects the Sun's rays and keeps it cool. The ancient Egyptians believed that scarab beetles were sacred.

Storage hump

A dromedary (Arabian camel) can go without water for a few weeks. Made up mostly of fat, its hump provides energy when food and water are scarce. The camel's long, thick eyelashes protect its eyes, and it can close its nostrils to keep out sand.

Addax
(*Addax nasomaculatus*)
Height at shoulder: up to 3 ft 9 in (1.15 m)
Horns: up to 3 ft 3 in (1 m)

MEDITERRANEAN SEA

KILOMETERS
0 200 400 600 800 1000
0 200 400 600
MILES

SANDFISH

SOOTY FALCON

LESSER EGYPTIAN JERBOA

Lake Nasser

Nile

RED SEA

ARABIAN PENINSULA

DESERT SCORPION

TIBESTI MTS

SAHARA

DESERT

SACRED SCARAB

The Sahara contains many rocky plateaus, called "hammadas."

Dromedary camel
(*Camelus dromedarius*)
Height at shoulder: up to 6 ft 6 in (2 m)
Body length: up to 11 ft (3.4 m)

Rare addax

Many addax have been killed for their skins, so they are now very rare. The addax never drinks—it gets moisture from eating plants. Its wide hooves allow it to travel quickly and easily over soft sand.

Fierce falcon

Sooty falcon chicks hatch in late summer, when many small birds migrate across the Sahara. Adult falcons catch migrating birds that stop to rest and feed them to their chicks.

Fat tail

If food is scarce, the spiny-tailed lizard can survive up to a month on the fat stored in its tail. If an enemy attacks, the agama runs headfirst into its burrow, sticks out its sharp, scaly tail, and beats it from side to side.

Rock climber

Barbary sheep live in the mountains of the Sahara. They are good at climbing on the rocky crags. They get most of the water they need from eating mountain plants, so they rarely need to drink.

Barbary sheep
(*Ammotragus lervia*)
Height at shoulder: up to 3 ft 7 in (1.1 m)
Horns: up to 2 ft 10 in (88 cm)

Sooty falcon
(*Falco concolor*)
Length: up to 14 in (36 cm)

North African spiny-tailed lizard (*Uromastyx acanthinura*)
Length including tail: up to 17 in (43 cm)

Rainforests and Lakes

THE TROPICAL RAINFORESTS of Africa stretch in a broad band from West Africa to the edge of the Great Rift Valley. This valley is a huge trough more than 4,000 miles (6,440 km) long. The valley floor has many lakes, which provide a rich habitat for wildlife.

The warm, humid environment of the rainforest is home to many animals, from okapis and forest birds to frogs, snakes, and insects. Many of the plant-eating animals feed on the leaves of shrubs beneath the giant forest trees. Leaves and fruits that fall to the forest floor decay rapidly, providing food for pigs, porcupines, and termites. Camouflage helps many animals hide from enemies and creep up on their prey without being seen. Unfortunately, large areas of rainforest have been destroyed for farming or building on, and many of the animals face possible extinction.

Armor plating

The pangolin is protected by hornlike scales, which act as a suit of armor. It uses its long tail as an extra hand, and can even hang from branches by the tip of its tail. The pangolin feeds on ants and termites, using its strong front legs to tear open their nests.

Common African pangolin
(*Manis tricuspis*)
Body length: up to 17 in (43 cm)
Tail: up to 2 ft (62 cm)

Royal antelope (*Neotragus pygmaeus*)
Body length: up to 1 ft 8 in (51 cm)
Height at shoulder: up to 10 in (26 cm)

Gentle giant

Gorillas are gentle vegetarians, and feed on leaves, stalks, bark, and fruits. They live in close-knit groups of up to 30 members, each led by an adult male. Gorillas communicate with one another using a wide range of sounds and gestures. Male gorillas over 10 years old have silvery-grey hair on their backs and are nicknamed "silverbacks."

Western gorilla
(*Gorilla gorilla*)
Body length: up to 3 ft 6 in (1 m)

Gaboon viper
(*Bitis gabonica*) Length: up to 6 ft 9 in (2 m)

Pencil legs

The tiny royal antelope is the size of a rabbit and its legs are as thin as pencils. It is the world's smallest antelope. When escaping from enemies, such as larger mammals, birds, and snakes, the royal antelope can leap as far as 9 ft (2.7 m) in one bound. It hides in the day and feeds at night.

Fearsome fangs

The gaboon viper is the world's heaviest venomous snake, with enough venom to kill 20 people. It also has the longest fangs—up to 2 in (5 cm) long—enabling it to inject venom deep into the bodies of its prey.

Powerful hunter

The leopard is so strong that it can drag the dead body of an animal weighing almost as much as itself. It stores large items of food in the branches of a tree to stop other animals from stealing its meals. The leopard's prey includes antelopes, monkeys, birds, fish, and snakes.

Okapi
(*Okapia johnstoni*)
Length: up to 6 ft 10 in (2.1 m)
Height at shoulder: 5 ft 7 in (1.7 m)

Stripey legs

The stripes on the okapi's legs help to hide it from enemies, such as the leopard, when it stands among the trees. It feeds on leaves, which it pulls from trees and bushes with its long tongue. The okapi's closest relation is the giraffe, which explains the male okapi's short, fur-covered horns.

Leopard
(*Panthera pardus*)
Body length: up to 6 ft 3 in (1.9 m)
Tail: up to 3 ft 3 in (1 m)

Black-casqued hornbill
(*Ceratogymna atrata*)
Length: up to
2 ft 4 in (70 cm)

Noisy feathers
As the black-casqued hornbill flies through the rainforest, its broad wings make a loud swishing noise. This is caused by air rushing through gaps between its flight feathers. The ridge along the top of its bill is called a casque.

Common hippopotamus
(*Hippopotamus amphibius*)
Body length: up to
16 ft 7 in (5 m)
Height at shoulder:
5 ft 5 in (1.65 m)

Open wide
Hippopotamuses spend most of the day resting in lakes and rivers, or on sand banks. They come out of the water at night to eat grass on lakeshores and riverbanks. A hippo can eat up to 180 lbs (80 kg) of plant material in one night. The hippo's webbed toes help it swim, and it can stay underwater for up to five minutes.

Chimpanzee
(*Pan troglodytes*)
Body length:
up to 3 ft 2 in
(96 cm)

African jacana
(*Actophilornis africanus*)
Length: up to 12 in (31 cm)

Tool user
The chimpanzee is very intelligent and is one of the few animals known to make and use tools. It breaks off twigs and uses them to fish termites out of their nest, and can also use a stone as a hammer. At night, it builds a nest of twigs and branches to sleep in.

Water walker
The African jacana's long toes help spread its weight and enable it to walk over floating water plants. The African jacana sometimes hides from enemies by sinking under the water, leaving only its bill and nostrils showing.

Goliath frog
(*Conraua goliath*)
Length: up to
12.6 in (32 cm)

Giant leaper
The goliath frog has long back legs and can travel more than 10 ft (3 m) in one leap. Its short front legs help absorb the impact of landing. Like all frogs, the goliath frog is a strong swimmer. Its long back legs and webbed feet push the frog through the water.

Super snail
The giant African snail eats all kinds of plants, using its rough tongue to scrape off bits of leaf. At the end of its long tentacles, it has simple eyes, which can tell light from dark. It uses the shorter tentacles to smell and feel.

Giant African snail
(*Achatina fulica*)
Length: up to 12 in (30 cm)

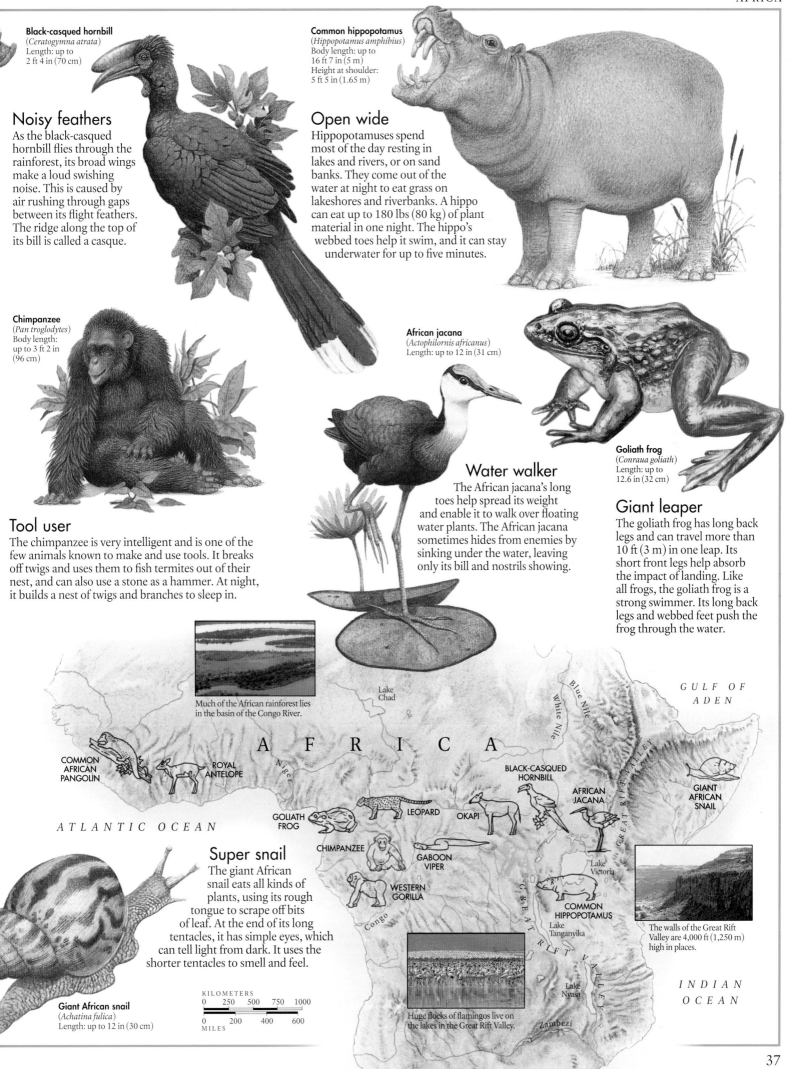

Much of the African rainforest lies in the basin of the Congo River.

The walls of the Great Rift Valley are 4,000 ft (1,250 m) high in places.

Huge flocks of flamingos live on the lakes in the Great Rift Valley.

KILOMETERS
0   250   500   750   1000

0   200   400   600
MILES

GULF OF ADEN

ATLANTIC OCEAN

AFRICA

COMMON AFRICAN PANGOLIN

ROYAL ANTELOPE

GOLIATH FROG

CHIMPANZEE

WESTERN GORILLA

LEOPARD

GABOON VIPER

OKAPI

BLACK-CASQUED HORNBILL

AFRICAN JACANA

COMMON HIPPOPOTAMUS

GIANT AFRICAN SNAIL

GREAT RIFT VALLEY

Niger

Congo

Lake Chad

White Nile

Blue Nile

Lake Victoria

Lake Tanganyika

Lake Nyasa

Zambezi

INDIAN OCEAN

The Savannah

THE SWEEPING GRASSLANDS of the African savannah are the last place on Earth where spectacular herds of large grazing animals still survive. There are two main seasons, wet and dry. At the start of the dry season, huge herds gather together and make long journeys to find fresh grass and water. The migrating herds sometimes fill the plains as far as the eye can see.

Grazing animals feed mainly on grass. Grasses can survive this onslaught because they can grow from the base of their leaf blades. This means they can easily regenerate, even when animals eat the top of the grass. The plant-eaters themselves are a source of food for the hunters of the savannah—lions, leopards, cheetahs, and wild dogs. After a kill, scavengers move in to clean up the leftovers. Lizards, snakes, and millions of insects also live in the grasses of the Savannah.

Bone cruncher

Hyenas have massive jaws that are strong enough to crunch through bones. They hunt in small groups at night, killing animals such as wildebeest and zebra by disembowelling them. They also eat animals killed by other hunters.

Spotted hyena
(*Crocuta crocuta*)
Height at shoulder: up to 2 ft 8 in (81 cm)
Body length: up to 6 ft (1.6 m)

Tireless trekker

Wildebeest trek hundreds of miles across the savannah searching for fresh grass. Whenever they stop to rest or graze, each male stakes out a territory, which he guards against other males. Baby wildebeest can run soon after they are born, and in a few hours they are able to keep up with the rest of the herd.

Super soldier

Within a termite colony, there are "soldiers" that defend the colony from attack by enemies. A soldier uses its head and strong jaws to stab and wound attackers.

South African termite
(*Macrotermes natalensis*)
Length: up to 0.55 in (1.4 cm)

Blue wildebeest
(*Connochaetes taurinus*)
Height at shoulder: up to 5 ft 1 in (1.6 m)
Body length: up to 7 ft 10 in (2.4 m)

Group protection

Zebras usually live in family groups, but in the dry season they gather in large herds. This helps protect them against enemies, since many pairs of eyes and ears are more likely to spot danger. Zebra stallions sometimes kick out at enemies, such as lions, and may smash their teeth.

Burchell's zebra
(*Equus quagga burchelli*)
Height at shoulder: up to 4 ft 7 in (1.4 m)
Body length: up to 8 ft (2.5 m)

African savannah elephant
(*Loxodonta africana*)
Height at shoulder: up to 13 ft 1 in (4 m)
Trunk: up to 6 ft 6 in (2 m)

Giant eaters

African savannah elephants spend up to 16 hours a day searching for enough food to support their bodies. A big male can weigh as much as 90 adult people. Elephants use their long trunks to reach leaves high on the trees, and are strong enough to push over trees to reach the top branches.

Cheetah
(*Acinonyx jubatus*)
Body length: up to 4 ft 9 in (1.45 m)
Tail: up to 2 ft 6 in (76 cm)

Lightning cat

The cheetah relies on short bursts of incredible speed to catch its prey. It can sprint at more than 62 mph (100 kph) over short distances, but tires easily. It grips the throat of its prey with its long canine teeth and uses its razor-sharp back teeth to slice meat off of bones.

ATLANTIC OCEAN

Congo

White-backed vulture
(*Gyps africanus*)
Length: up to
3 ft 1 in (84 cm)
Wingspan:
up to 7 ft 3 in
(2.2 m)

Naked neck
The naked head and neck of the white-backed vulture make it easier for the bird to poke its head inside the carcass of a dead animal when feeding. Vultures soar high above the savannah and use their keen eyesight to search for dead animals.

Fast runner
In spite of its size, the black rhino is very agile and can gallop at 30 mph (48 kph) over short distances. It uses its hooklike upper lip to pull bark and leaves from vegetation.

KILOMETERS
0   200   400   600

0   200   400
MILES

Black rhinoceros
(*Diceros bicornis*)
Body length: up to
12 ft 6 in (3.8 m)
Front horn: up to 4 ft 3 in
(130 cm)

Gathering rainclouds indicate the start of the wet season in the Ngorongoro Crater, Tanzania.

WHITE-BACKED VULTURE

Lake Victoria

CHEETAH

THOMSON'S GAZELLE

Lake Tanganyika

AFRICAN SAVANNAH ELEPHANT

NORTHERN RED-HEADED WEAVER

Lake Nyasa (Lake Malawi)

BLACK RHINO

A F R I C A

GREAT RIFT VALLEY

INDIAN OCEAN

SPOTTED HYENA

LION

Zambezi

BURCHELL'S ZEBRA

GIRAFFE

BLUE WILDEBEEST

A large herd of wildebeest migrate across the Tanzanian plain.

KALAHARI DESERT

SOUTH AFRICAN TERMITE

Acacias are one of the most common savannah trees.

Lion (*Panthera leo*)
Height at shoulder:
up to 4 ft (1.2 m)
Body length: up to
8 ft 4 in (2.5 m)

Sleepy hunter
Lions live in family groups called "prides," made up of female relatives and their young, and one or more adult males. Lions hunt at night and sleep for about 21 hours a day. Their roars can be heard up to 5 miles (8 km) away.

Tree height
The giraffe's extra-long neck allows it to reach leaves and twigs 20 ft (6 m) above the ground. The giraffe uses its long tongue and curled upper lip to strip the leaves from branches.

Giraffe
(*Giraffa camelopardalis*)
Height to head:
up to 19 ft 8 in (6 m)
Neck: up to 8 ft (2.4 m)

Jumping gazelle
Thomson's gazelles live in herds. If they sense danger, the herd may spring up and down with their heads and legs held stiffly and their bodies curved. This is called "pronking" or "stotting" and can confuse enemies.

Thomson's gazelle
(*Eudorcas thomsonii*)
Height at shoulder: up to
2 ft 6 in (76 cm)
Horns: up to 17 in (44 cm)

Nest weaver
The male red-headed weaver bird uses supple green twigs to weave an elaborate nest that helps attract a female. The nest is usually fixed at the end of a twig to protect it, with thick walls to keep the chicks cool by day and warm at night.

Northern red-headed weaver
(*Anaplectes leuconotos*)
Length: up to 6 in
(15 cm)

Madagascar

MADAGASCAR is the fourth largest island in the world. It was once attached to mainland Africa, but it split off and drifted away tens of millions of years ago. This long period of isolation has allowed many unique animals to develop there, including tenrecs, lemurs, and two-thirds of the world's chameleons. In contrast, some common animal groups, such as woodpeckers and venomous snakes, do not occur on the island at all.

One of the reasons for the wide range of wildlife on Madagascar is its varied climate and vegetation. The east coast has a tropical rainforest, but the extreme south of the island is drier, with semidesert conditions. Mountains run down the island, and the high central plateau is relatively cold, covered with grassy savannah.

Common sunbird-asity
(*Neodrepanis coruscans*)
Length: up to 4 in (10.5 cm)

Sugar straw
The common sunbird-asity uses its long, curved beak to reach the nectar inside flowers, and laps it up with the brush-like tip of its tongue. As it feeds, it carries pollen from one flower to the next and helps pollinate them. In the mating season, the male sunbird-asity develops bare blue skin on the sides of his head, probably to attract females for mating.

Verreaux's sifaka
(*Propithecus verreauxi*)
Body length: up to 19 in (48 cm)
Tail: up to 24 in (60 cm)

Strange call
The sifaka's name comes from the strange call it makes to warn other sifakas of danger—"shi-fakh! shi-fakh!" The sifaka's legs are much longer than its arms and help it make amazing leaps of more than 16 ft (5 m) through the trees. The sifaka comes down to the ground occasionally and hops on its back feet with its arms waving wildly over its head. It cannot run on all fours; its arms are too short.

Ring-tailed lemur
(*Lemur catta*)
Body length: up to 18 in (46 cm)
Tail: up to 29 in (63 cm)

Smelly signals
The ring-tailed lemur produces a scent, which it uses to mark its territory and tell rival lemurs to keep out. The male ring-tail also uses his scent in "stink fights" with other males. He spreads scent from the glands on his wrists and armpits over his tail, then shakes his tail over his back to fan the smell toward his rival. Lemurs feed on fruit, leaves, tree bark, and grass.

Largest litter
The female tail-less tenrec produces the largest litter of any mammal—up to 32 young. Only about 16–20 usually survive. To frighten away enemies, the tenrec raises the spines and stiff hair on its head and back, stamps its front feet, hisses, and opens its mouth wide.

Tail-less tenrec
(*Tenrec ecaudatus*)
Body length: up to 14 in (35 cm)

Clever climber
The fosa's tail is almost as long as its body, and helps it balance when climbing trees. Its prey includes lemurs and other mammals, birds, reptiles, and insects. The fosa is the most widespread carnivore on Madagascar, although when humans introduced cats and dogs to the island, they also exposed the fosa to diseases.

Fosa
(*Cryptoprocta ferox*)
Body length: up to 2 ft 8 in (80 cm)
Tail: up to 2 ft 3 in (70 cm)

Aye-aye
(*Daubentonia madagascariensis*)
Head and body: up to 15 in (37 cm)
Tail: up to 21 in (53 cm)

Oversized ears
The forest-dwelling aye-aye is a type of lemur with huge, bat-like ears. Its hearing is so good that it can detect insects moving beneath the bark of trees. It uses its long, spindly middle finger to pull out juicy grubs, and also eats plant food, such as nuts, bamboo shoots, and fruit. The aye-aye is endangered due to the destruction of its habitat.

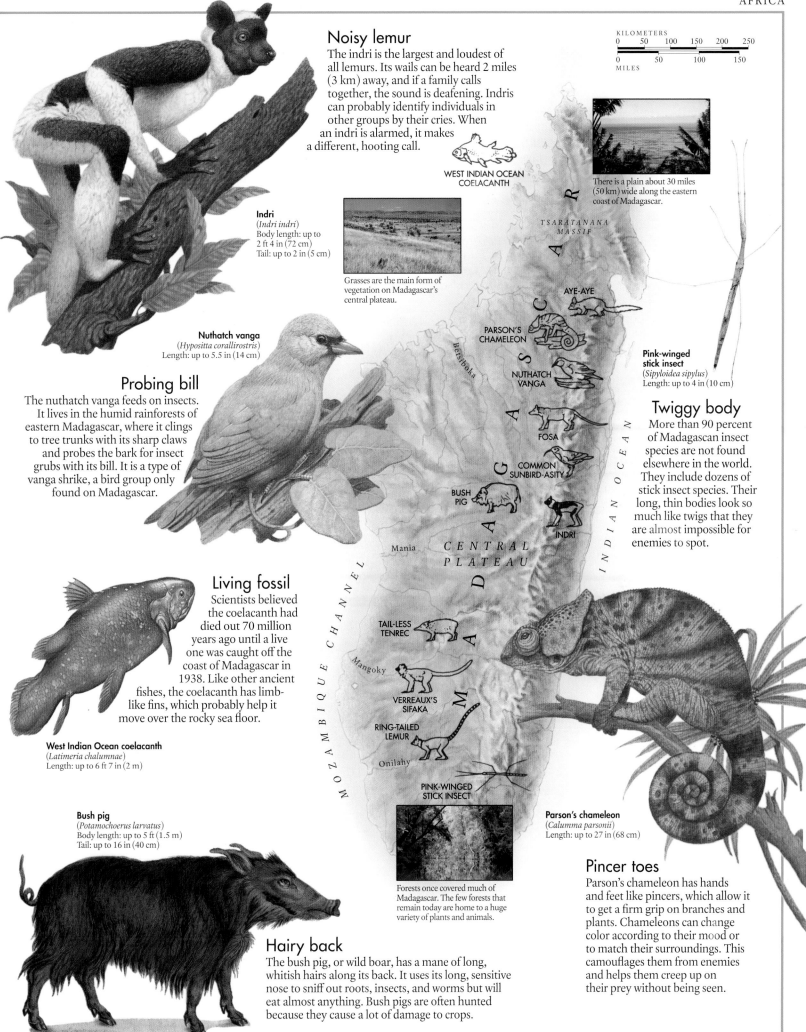

Noisy lemur

The indri is the largest and loudest of all lemurs. Its wails can be heard 2 miles (3 km) away, and if a family calls together, the sound is deafening. Indris can probably identify individuals in other groups by their cries. When an indri is alarmed, it makes a different, hooting call.

WEST INDIAN OCEAN COELACANTH

There is a plain about 30 miles (50 km) wide along the eastern coast of Madagascar.

Indri
(*Indri indri*)
Body length: up to 2 ft 4 in (72 cm)
Tail: up to 2 in (5 cm)

Grasses are the main form of vegetation on Madagascar's central plateau.

Probing bill

The nuthatch vanga feeds on insects. It lives in the humid rainforests of eastern Madagascar, where it clings to tree trunks with its sharp claws and probes the bark for insect grubs with its bill. It is a type of vanga shrike, a bird group only found on Madagascar.

Nuthatch vanga
(*Hypositta corallirostris*)
Length: up to 5.5 in (14 cm)

Twiggy body

More than 90 percent of Madagascan insect species are not found elsewhere in the world. They include dozens of stick insect species. Their long, thin bodies look so much like twigs that they are almost impossible for enemies to spot.

Pink-winged stick insect
(*Sipyloidea sipylus*)
Length: up to 4 in (10 cm)

Living fossil

Scientists believed the coelacanth had died out 70 million years ago until a live one was caught off the coast of Madagascar in 1938. Like other ancient fishes, the coelacanth has limb-like fins, which probably help it move over the rocky sea floor.

West Indian Ocean coelacanth
(*Latimeria chalumnae*)
Length: up to 6 ft 7 in (2 m)

Bush pig
(*Potamochoerus larvatus*)
Body length: up to 5 ft (1.5 m)
Tail: up to 16 in (40 cm)

Forests once covered much of Madagascar. The few forests that remain today are home to a huge variety of plants and animals.

Hairy back

The bush pig, or wild boar, has a mane of long, whitish hairs along its back. It uses its long, sensitive nose to sniff out roots, insects, and worms but will eat almost anything. Bush pigs are often hunted because they cause a lot of damage to crops.

Pincer toes

Parson's chameleon has hands and feet like pincers, which allow it to get a firm grip on branches and plants. Chameleons can change color according to their mood or to match their surroundings. This camouflages them from enemies and helps them creep up on their prey without being seen.

Parson's chameleon
(*Calumma parsonii*)
Length: up to 27 in (68 cm)

Map labels:
KILOMETERS 0 50 100 150 200 250
MILES 0 50 100 150

TSARATANANA MASSIF
AYE-AYE
PARSON'S CHAMELEON
Betsiboka
NUTHATCH VANGA
FOSA
COMMON SUNBIRD-ASITY
BUSH PIG
INDRI
Mania
CENTRAL PLATEAU
MOZAMBIQUE CHANNEL
INDIAN OCEAN
MADAGASCAR
TAIL-LESS TENREC
Mangoky
VERREAUX'S SIFAKA
RING-TAILED LEMUR
Onilahy
PINK-WINGED STICK INSECT

Siberia

THE CONIFER FORESTS OF SIBERIA in northern Asia make up the largest area of forest in the world. The cones of the larch, fir, and spruce trees that grow there provide a vital source of food for animals, especially during the winter. South of the forests lies Lake Baikal. This lake has been isolated for millions of years, and many animals there are not found anywhere else in the world. North of the forest belt lies the barren Arctic wastes, or tundra. During the tundra winter, which lasts for nine months each year, many animals move south to the shelter of the conifer forests. The brief tundra summer is a time of plenty, when it is light for 24 hours a day.

Warning howl

Wolves live in groups called packs. They howl to keep in touch with each other or to warn rival packs to keep away. Packs have a strict social order, and wolves use body language to signal their rank within the pack. For example, a low-ranking wolf would lie on its back, with its ears pulled back and its tail between its legs.

Gray wolf (*Canis lupus*)
Body length: up to 4 ft 3 in (1.3 m)
Tail: up to 20 in (52 cm)

Trumpet call

The whooper swan is one of the noisiest swans in the world. It gets its name from its loud, trumpeting call, which can be heard over great distances. Its wings also make a swishing sound when it flies. Whooper swans breed in the tundra regions and on lakes deep in the conifer forests.

Whooper swan (*Cygnus cygnus*)
Wingspan: up to 5 ft 5 in (1.65 m)

Unique seal

The Baikal seal is the only seal that lives in fresh water. It is related to the ringed seals that live in the Arctic Ocean. Millions of years ago, its ancestors probably swam from this ocean up the River Lena to reach Lake Baikal. The Baikal seal feeds on fish, snapping them up with its sharp teeth.

Baikal seal
(*Pusa sibirica*)
Length: up to
4 ft 9 in (1.45 m)

Wax droplets

The waxwing is named after the red dots on its wings, which look like drops of wax. It feeds on fruit and insects, and relies mainly on berries in winter. The waxwing digests its food quickly—seeds can pass through its digestive system in as little as 16 minutes.

Bohemian waxwing
(*Bombycilla garrulus*)
Length: up to 9 in (23 cm)

ARCTIC OCEAN

BERING SEA

EAST SIBERIAN SEA

ARCTIC GROUND SQUIRREL

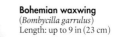

KILOMETERS
0   250   500   750   1000
0   150   300   450   600
MILES

NOVOSIBIRSKIYE OSTROVA

LAPTEV SEA

SEVERNAYA ZEMLYA

BARENTS SEA

NOVAYA ZEMLYA

KARA SEA

Indigirka

SIBERIAN LEMMING

Lena

KAMCHATKA PENINSULA

SABLE

SIBERIAN TIT

SNOWY OWL

SIBERIAN JAY

SEA OF OKHOTSK

Ob

REINDEER

S I B E R I A

HAZEL GROUSE

GREY WOLF

BOHEMIAN WAXWING

Angara

SAKHALIN

Yenisei

Lena

Lake Baikal is the deepest and oldest lake on Earth. It also contains more water than any other lake.

The huge expanses of Siberian forests cover an area one-third larger than the United States.

WHOOPER SWAN

BAIKAL SEAL

Lake Baikal

Powerful hunter

The huge and powerful snowy owl glides silently over the frozen tundra searching for lemmings and voles to eat. It can catch up to 10 lemmings in one day and is strong enough to catch and kill hares. Its white and black speckled plumage camouflages it against the snow, and the thick feathers on its legs keep it warm.

Snowy owl
(*Bubo scandiacus*)
Length: up to
2 ft 1 in (64 cm)
Wingspan: up to
5 ft 5 in (1.65 m)

Snowshoe hooves

The reindeer, or caribou, has broad hooves that help it walk in deep snow. It also uses its hooves to scrape away snow to eat lichen and moss. Some reindeer migrate between summer breeding grounds on the tundra and winter feeding grounds in the forests. Unlike other deer, the male and the female both have antlers.

Reindeer
(*Rangifer tarandus*)
Body length: up to
7 ft 2 in (2.2 m)
Tail: up to
8 in (21 cm)

Siberian lemming
(*Lemmus sibiricus*)
Length: up to
6 in (16 cm)

On the move

Every three or four years, the number of lemmings grows so much that thousands leave their nests to find new homes. Once they are on the move, lemmings do not stop, even in big towns or at busy roads. Many are eaten or die from exhaustion or starvation. Others drown trying to cross rivers, lakes, or the sea.

Underground larders

The Arctic ground squirrel stores food in its underground burrow during the short summer period. It makes several "larders" of food to last it through its winter sleep, or hibernation, and eats a lot in the summer to build up stores of body fat. If the ground squirrel senses danger, it makes a loud call to warn others.

Arctic ground squirrel
(*Spermophilus parryi*)
Body: up to 10.5 in (27 cm)
Tail: up to 4 in (11 cm)

Speckled feathers

The brown, speckled markings on the feathers of the female hazel grouse help hide her from enemies while she is sitting on her eggs. The hazel grouse has large flight muscles, which also act as a store of food. Grouse are the most common and widespread birds in the conifer forests.

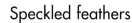

Hazel grouse (*Bonasa bonasia*)
Length: up to 15.8 in (40 cm)

Siberian tit
(*Poecile cinctus*)
Length: up to
5.5 in (14 cm)

Fur coat

The sable has a beautiful, thick coat and was hunted almost to extinction for its fur. Some have been reared in captivity and released back into the wild, so the sable is no longer an endangered species. It feeds on small mammals, such as voles, as well as fish, insects, nuts, and berries. It has well-developed scent glands and uses this scent to mark the edges of its territory.

Sable (*Martes zibellina*)
Body length: up to 22 in (56 cm)
Tail: up to 7.5 in (19 cm)

Cone eater

The Siberian jay uses its strong beak to break open tree cones and reach the seeds inside. The number of Siberian jays are closely linked to the number of cones on the trees—when there are few cones, their numbers fall dramatically. When food is in short supply, they move into towns and villages in search of scraps.

Siberian jay
(*Perisoreus infaustus*)
Length: up to 12 in (31 cm)

Energy saver

The Siberian tit stays in the forests year round, despite the freezing winter temperatures. At night, its heartbeat and other body processes slow down, and its temperature drops so that it uses up less energy. This helps it survive when energy-giving food is hard to find.

Deserts and Steppe

A VAST AREA OF GRASSLAND, called the steppe, stretches across the southern part of Russia and into China. The climate in this region consists of very hot summers and long, icy winters, with cold winds blowing down from the frozen north. Huge herds of grazing animals, such as saigas and onagers, once populated the steppe, but these have been almost wiped out by hunting. Some of the remaining herds are now protected, but they are forced to live in drier areas, away from farms.

South of the steppe lie the deserts of central Asia, where rainfall is less than 12 in (30 cm) a year. Summers are baking hot, but at night the temperature can drop by as much as 36°F (20°C). Some desert animals sleep through the summer months; some come out only at night. Others have adapted to survive without drinking.

Bactrian camel
(*Camelus bactrianus*)
Height at shoulder: up to 5 ft 11 in (1.8 m)
Body length: up to 11 ft 6 in (3.5 m)

Two humps

Unlike the Arabian camel, the bactrian camel has two humps. In winter it grows long, shaggy hair that keeps it warm, but in summer most of this hair falls out. It has wide, flat feet that enable it to walk over the soft sand without sinking in. A small number of wild bactrian camels live in the Gobi Desert.

Rare eagle

The rare steppe eagle nests on the ground because there are so few trees on the steppe grasslands. It is a fierce hunter, swooping down out of the sky to seize its prey with its strong, sharp talons. It then uses its hooked beak to tear its food into bite-sized pieces.

Steppe eagle (*Aquila nipalensis*)
Body length: up to 2 ft 8 in (81 cm)
Wingspan: up to 7 ft (2.1 m)

Asiatic wild ass
(*Equus hemionus*)
Height at shoulder: up to 4 ft 3 in (1.3 m)
Body length: up to 8 ft 2 in (2.5 m)

Lebetine viper
(*Macrovipera lebetina*)
Length: up to 7 ft 6 in (2.3 m)

Lethal viper

The venomous lebetine viper is one of the largest desert snakes. It lies in wait to ambush the rodents and lizards on which it feeds, then injects venom into its prey through its long, hollow fangs. The viper waits for its victim to die and then swallows it whole. It hunts at night and rests in the shade or below ground during the heat of the day.

Fast runner

The Asiatic wild ass, or onager, can run at speeds of 40 mph (65 kph) or more—as fast as any racehorse. It can go for two or three days without drinking, which helps it survive in the dry conditions of the deserts and steppe. In summer it lives on the high grassland, but in winter it moves to lower levels for the fresh grass.

Cheek pouches

The hamster feeds on seeds, grain, roots, plants, and insects. In late summer, it stores large supplies of food in a network of tunnels that it digs beneath the steppe, carrying food in special cheek pouches. Hamsters have been known to store as much as 143 lb (65 kg) of food. The hamster hibernates in its burrow in winter, occasionally waking to eat.

Desert monitor
(*Varanus griseus*)
Length: up to 4 ft 3 in (1.3 m)

Giant lizard

The huge monitor lizard, or varan, eats almost anything, from other lizards and tortoises to rodents and birds. Sometimes it even eats its own young. It swallows its prey whole, like a snake. To frighten enemies away, the monitor lizard hisses loudly and lashes its powerful tail from side to side.

Common hamster
(*Cricetus cricetus*)
Body length: up to 12.6 in (32 cm)
Tail: up to 2.7 in (6.8 cm)

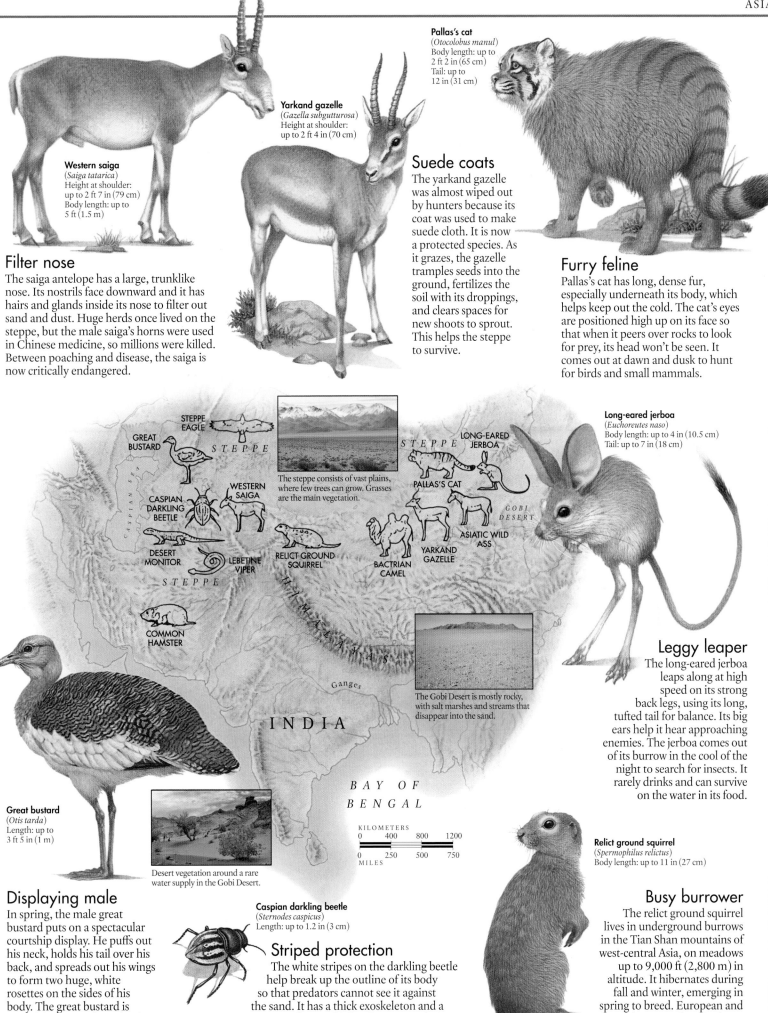

Western saiga
(*Saiga tatarica*)
Height at shoulder:
up to 2 ft 7 in (79 cm)
Body length: up to
5 ft (1.5 m)

Yarkand gazelle
(*Gazella subgutturosa*)
Height at shoulder:
up to 2 ft 4 in (70 cm)

Pallas's cat
(*Otocolobus manul*)
Body length: up to
2 ft 2 in (65 cm)
Tail: up to
12 in (31 cm)

Filter nose
The saiga antelope has a large, trunklike nose. Its nostrils face downward and it has hairs and glands inside its nose to filter out sand and dust. Huge herds once lived on the steppe, but the male saiga's horns were used in Chinese medicine, so millions were killed. Between poaching and disease, the saiga is now critically endangered.

Suede coats
The yarkand gazelle was almost wiped out by hunters because its coat was used to make suede cloth. It is now a protected species. As it grazes, the gazelle tramples seeds into the ground, fertilizes the soil with its droppings, and clears spaces for new shoots to sprout. This helps the steppe to survive.

Furry feline
Pallas's cat has long, dense fur, especially underneath its body, which helps keep out the cold. The cat's eyes are positioned high up on its face so that when it peers over rocks to look for prey, its head won't be seen. It comes out at dawn and dusk to hunt for birds and small mammals.

STEPPE
EAGLE

GREAT
BUSTARD

S T E P P E

CASPIAN
DARKLING
BEETLE

WESTERN
SAIGA

DESERT
MONITOR

LEBETINE
VIPER

S T E P P E

COMMON
HAMSTER

RELICT GROUND
SQUIRREL

S T E P P E

LONG-EARED
JERBOA

PALLAS'S CAT

G O B I
D E S E R T

BACTRIAN
CAMEL

YARKAND
GAZELLE

ASIATIC WILD
ASS

The steppe consists of vast plains, where few trees can grow. Grasses are the main vegetation.

Long-eared jerboa
(*Euchoreutes naso*)
Body length: up to 4 in (10.5 cm)
Tail: up to 7 in (18 cm)

H I M A L A Y A S

Ganges

I N D I A

The Gobi Desert is mostly rocky, with salt marshes and streams that disappear into the sand.

Leggy leaper
The long-eared jerboa leaps along at high speed on its strong back legs, using its long, tufted tail for balance. Its big ears help it hear approaching enemies. The jerboa comes out of its burrow in the cool of the night to search for insects. It rarely drinks and can survive on the water in its food.

Great bustard
(*Otis tarda*)
Length: up to
3 ft 5 in (1 m)

B A Y   O F
B E N G A L

KILOMETERS
0   400   800   1200

0   250   500   750
MILES

Desert vegetation around a rare water supply in the Gobi Desert.

Displaying male
In spring, the male great bustard puts on a spectacular courtship display. He puffs out his neck, holds his tail over his back, and spreads out his wings to form two huge, white rosettes on the sides of his body. The great bustard is one of the largest flying birds, but it usually walks or runs.

Caspian darkling beetle
(*Sternodes caspicus*)
Length: up to 1.2 in (3 cm)

Striped protection
The white stripes on the darkling beetle help break up the outline of its body so that predators cannot see it against the sand. It has a thick exoskeleton and a compact shape, which reduces water loss and helps the beetle survive the heat.

Relict ground squirrel
(*Spermophilus relictus*)
Body length: up to 11 in (27 cm)

Busy burrower
The relict ground squirrel lives in underground burrows in the Tian Shan mountains of west-central Asia, on meadows up to 9,000 ft (2,800 m) in altitude. It hibernates during fall and winter, emerging in spring to breed. European and Asian ground squirrels are sometimes called susliks.

The Himalayas

THE HIMALAYAS are a gigantic chain of mountains that stretch right across northern India—a distance of about 1,500 miles (2,400 km). The Himalayas contain many of the highest mountains in the world; snow and ice cover many of the peaks year round. The mountain chain separates the cool Asian lands to the north from the tropical regions of northern India. There are a wide variety of different habitats in the Himalayas: tropical forests in the foothills, rhododendron and bamboo forests and grassy meadows higher up, and bleak tundra areas below the high peaks.

Only insects can survive at the high altitudes of the mountain peaks. They feed on plant spores, pollen, and other insects, which are swept up from the Indian plains by the strong winds. Most animals live farther down the slopes in the forests and meadows. The mountain animals have thick fur and large lungs to help them survive the cold, wind, and thin air. Many animals move down to the snow-free lower slopes and valleys in winter, while others hibernate instead.

Graceful leaper
The Hanuman langur is a graceful monkey that can leap up to 30 ft (9 m) through the trees. It feeds on young leaves, fruit, and flowers and has a complex stomach and ridged teeth to help it digest its tough food. Named after Hanuman, the Hindu monkey god, it is a sacred animal in India.

Hanuman langur
(*Semnopithecus entellus*)
Body length: up to 2 ft 7 in (78 cm)
Tail: up to 3 ft 8 in (1.1 m)

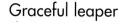

Bhutan glory (*Bhutanitis lidderdalii*) Wingspan: up to 4.3 in (11 cm)

Hidden colors
The Bhutan glory flies at altitudes of 5,000–9,000 ft (1,500–2,700 m) in the Himalayan forests. Its dark wings blend in among the shade of the trees. When it rains, the butterfly rests with its wings folded, hiding the bright colors on its hindwings.

Blood pheasant
(*Ithaginis cruentus*)
Length: up to 19 in (48 cm)

High hunter
The powerful snow leopard, or ounce, feeds on wild sheep and goats, which it hunts up to 18,000 ft (5,500 m) up in the mountains. In winter, it follows its prey down into the forests. The snow leopard can make huge leaps over ravines. It has long, thick fur to help it keep warm and broad feet that keep it from sinking into the snow.

Snow leopard
(*Panthera uncia*)
Body length: up to 4 ft 1 in (1.25 m)
Tail: up to 3 ft 5 in (1 m)

Red stripes
The blood pheasant is named after the bright red stripes on the male's feathers, which help him to attract a female for mating. The female bird has brown feathers, which help to camouflage her while she sits on her eggs. Blood pheasants make their nests in grass-lined gaps between large boulders. They eat pine shoots, mosses, ferns, and lichens.

Siberian ibex
(*Capra sibirica*)
Height at shoulder: up to 3 ft 5 in (1 m)

Huge horns
The male Siberian ibex has huge horns, which he uses in spectacular "head-butting" contests to fight rival males. The ibex leaps around on the rocky crags where it is safe from most enemies. Its thick coat helps it survive the cold, but it also migrates to the lower slopes in winter.

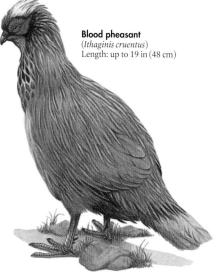

The grassy meadows on the lower mountain slopes provide food for many grazing animals.

Mount Everest, the highest mountain in the world, is one of the Himalayan peaks.

KILOMETERS
0   100   200   300   400

0   100   200   300
MILES

Corkscrew horns

The markhor is a wild goat with huge curly horns that can grow up to 4 ft (1.2 m) long. Male and female animals both have horns, but the female's are smaller. The markhor's coat is short and smooth in summer but grows longer in winter to keep out the cold. It also moves down the mountains to find warmer places in winter. Once nearly extinct, markhor numbers are now increasing again.

Markhor
(*Capra falconeri*)
Body length: up to
5 ft 7 in (1.7 m)
Tail: up to 7.8 in (20 cm)

Fire bird

The fire-tailed myzornis has red markings on its wings and tail, making it look as if it is on fire. This tiny bird lives in the evergreen mountain forests of Nepal. It feeds on insects, spiders, berries, tree sap, and nectar, which it laps up with its bristly tongue.

Fire-tailed myzornis
(*Myzornis pyrrhoura*)
Wingspan: up to 5 in (13 cm)

Winter sleep

The Himalayan marmot hibernates in its burrow in winter. They live in groups. One always stands guard to warn the others of any danger. Marmots feed on plants and come out in the early morning to find food.

Himalayan marmot
(*Marmota himalayana*)
Body length: up to 2 ft 2 in (65 cm)
Tail: up to 6 in (15 cm)

Takin
(*Budorcas taxicolor*)
Body length: up to 7 ft 2 in (2.2 m)
Tail: up to 8.7 in (22 cm)

Sturdy legs

The takin has thick, strong legs and large hooves, which help it climb the steep slopes. In summer, herds live high up the mountains in rhododendron and bamboo thickets. In winter, they move down to the valleys. Young takin can follow their mother over the slopes at just three days old.

Himalayan black bear
(*Ursus thibetanus laniger*)
Body length: up to
6 ft 3 in (1.9 m)

Furry fringe

The yak has a very long, furry coat that reaches almost to the ground. Under the long hairs is a layer of short, dense underfur, which insulates the yak from the freezing winter temperatures. It molts this underfur in the spring. The yak is nimble, despite its size. It lives in the Tibetan plateau, in grasslands, tundra, and desert.

Yak (*Bos mutus*)
Height at shoulder: up to 6 ft 8 in (2 m)
Body length: up to 12 ft 6 in (3.8 m)

Moving bear

The Himalayan black bear lives in the forests on the lower slopes of the mountains. It can climb well and is a good swimmer. Sometimes it curls into a ball and rolls downhill. During winter months, it moves to the foothills where food is available year round.

FIRE-TAILED
MYZORNIS

BLOOD
PHEASANT   TAKIN

BHUTAN
GLORY

SNOW LEOPARD

A   Y   A

Ganges

Himalayan griffon vulture
(*Gyps himalayensis*)
Wingspan: up to 9 ft 6 in (2.9 m)

Trees on the mountainsides soak up rain and help hold the soil together.

Bone stripper

The harsh life in the mountains provides a plentiful supply of dead animals for the huge Himalayan griffon vulture to eat. A group of these vultures can strip a small animal, such as an antelope, to the bone in only 20 minutes.

BAY OF
BENGAL

47

The Far East

CHINA IS ONE OF THE LARGEST COUNTRIES in the world. The climate over this vast area is controlled by the wet summer monsoon winds and the bitterly cold winds that blow down from the Arctic in winter. Mountains or desert cover two-thirds of the country, with tropical rainforests in the south. These habitats provide a refuge for some of the world's rarest animals, such as the giant panda and the Siberian tiger. The islands of Japan stretch for more than 1,200 miles (1,900 km) off the east coast of China. Japan has a mild climate, with warm summers, cool winters, and plentiful rainfall. Broadleaved forests cover much of the land.

Japanese macaque (*Macaca fuscata*)
Length: up to 2 ft 2 in (65 cm)
Tail: up to 3.4 in (8.7 cm)

Hot baths

Japanese macaque monkeys live in troops of up to 40 individuals, led by an adult male. Troops that live in the cold, snowy mountains of northern Japan have learned to keep warm in winter by taking hot baths in the volcanic mountain springs. They sit in the springs with hot water right up to their necks. Other troops of this intelligent monkey have learned to wash their food before eating it.

Sika deer
(*Cervus nippon*)
Height at shoulder:
up to 3 ft 9 in (115 cm)

Bamboo eater

The giant panda feeds mainly on bamboo, spending up to 16 hours a day eating about 600 bamboo stems. Each giant panda lives in its own territory in the misty mountain forests of southwest China. Its thick, waterproof fur helps keep it warm and dry. Baby pandas are pink, blind, and helpless when they are born. They take their first steps at about three months old, but cannot walk well until they are a year old.

Giant panda
(*Ailuropoda melanoleuca*)
Body length: up to 5 ft 11 in (1.8 m)
Tail: up to 6 in (16 cm)

Warning signal

The sika deer has a patch of white fur on its rump that it fluffs up when it is alarmed, acting as a warning signal to others. In summer, the sika deer has a chestnut coat with white spots, which helps camouflage it among the trees. In winter, it grows darker fur and loses most of its spots. Sika deer are hardy animals and have been introduced to forests all over the world.

Golden pheasant
(*Chrysolophus pictus*)
Length: up to 3 ft 9 in (1.15 m)

Baiji (*Lipotes vexillifer*)
Length: up to 8 ft 4 in (2.5 m)

Northern treeshrew
(*Tupaia belangeri*)
Head and body:
up to 9 in (23 cm)
Tail: up to 7.9 in (20 cm)

Courting collar

The male golden pheasant has a brightly colored collar of feathers that he displays to attract a female during courtship. Golden pheasants live in the forests of central China. They nest on the ground, and the female sits on the eggs to keep them warm. The chicks can feed themselves as soon as they hatch, and can fly from about a week old.

Dinosaur days

The treeshrew probably looks like the very first mammals that developed millions of years ago, in the days of the dinosaurs. Treeshrews live in pairs, building a nest on the ground or among tree roots. The male marks his territory with a strong scent made by glands in his throat.

Echo-sounder

The baiji, or Chinese river dolphin, is one of the few species of dolphins that live in freshwater. It has poor eyesight and finds its food by sending out high-pitched sounds and waiting for the echo to bounce back. The time this takes helps the baiji figure out how near objects are. It also probes in the mud with its long snout to look for shrimp. The baiji is so rare, it may even be extinct.

Climbing panda

The red panda uses its sharp claws to climb quickly through the trees. It feeds mainly on bamboo shoots, roots, grasses, and fruit. The panda often washes itself like a cat, licking a foot and then wiping the wet foot over its fur.

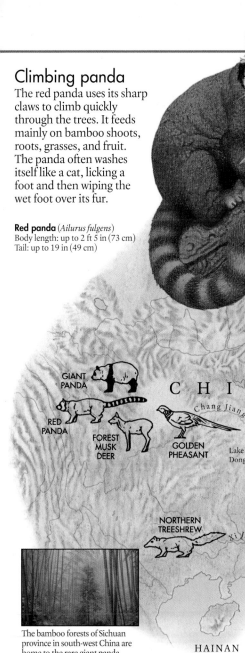

Red panda (*Ailurus fulgens*)
Body length: up to 2 ft 5 in (73 cm)
Tail: up to 19 in (49 cm)

The Huang He, or Yellow River, flows right across China. It contains a lot of silt, which gives the water a yellowish color.

SIBERIAN TIGER

SIKA DEER

JAPANESE MACAQUE

PACIFIC OCEAN

SEA OF JAPAN

J A P A N

JAPANESE GIANT SALAMANDER

Japanese giant salamander
(*Andrias japonicus*)
Length: up to 5 ft (1.5 m)

K O R E A N P E N I N S U L A

C H I N A

GIANT PANDA

RED PANDA

FOREST MUSK DEER

GOLDEN PHEASANT

Chang Jiang

Lake Dongting

Lake Poyang

NORTHERN TREESHREW

Xi Jiang

CHINESE ALLIGATOR

EAST CHINA SEA

BAIJI

Huang He

Mountainous forest covers about 70 percent of Japan's land area.

TAIWAN

Siberian tiger
(*Panthera tigris altaica*)
Body length: up to 9 ft 6 in (2.9 m)
Tail: up to 3 ft 7 in (109 cm)

SOUTH CHINA SEA

HAINAN

The bamboo forests of Sichuan province in south-west China are home to the rare giant panda.

Giant from the past

The huge Japanese giant salamander is the second-largest living amphibian, after the Chinese salamander. Amphibians like this lived on Earth about 300 million years ago. The giant salamander lives in cold streams, using a flap of skin along the sides of its body to take in oxygen from the water. It also comes to the surface to take air into its lungs.

Largest cat

The Siberian tiger is the largest and rarest big cat. It is larger, furrier, and paler than tigers in India and Indonesia. Tigers live alone, marking their territories with scent, droppings, and scrape marks. They also roar to tell other tigers to keep away. A tiger's roars can be heard up to 2 miles (3 km) away. There are probably only a few hundred Siberian tigers left in the wild.

Smelly stomach

The male musk deer has a gland under its stomach that produces a smelly substance called musk in the breeding season. Humans have killed many musk deer for this gland, which is used to make perfume. The male deer has canine teeth about 3 in (7 cm) long, which stick out of the sides of his mouth. In the breeding season, males fight each other with these teeth.

Forest musk deer
(*Moschus berezovskii*)
Body: up to 2 ft 8 in (80 cm)
Tail: up to 1.6 in (4 cm)

Chinese alligator
(*Alligator sinensis*)
Length: up to 7 ft 2 in (2.2 m)

Rare reptile

The timid Chinese alligator sleeps or hibernates in caves or burrows during the cold, dry winter months. It comes out in spring to mate and raise a family. This alligator feeds on snails, clams, rats, and insects. Today there are probably less than 200 of these alligators left due to the destruction of their habitat and collection by humans. They are found only in the lower part of the Chang Jiang river in eastern China.

KILOMETERS
0 150 300 450 600

0 100 200 300 400
MILES

Southeastern Asia and India

THE CLIMATE IN INDIA is dominated by the seasonal changes caused by the monsoon winds. They bring torrential rain and violent storms in summer. Dry, cooler weather occurs in winter. There are many types of habitats in India, from mangrove swamps along the coasts, to open plains, scrubland, and broadleaved forests inland. India is a meeting place for animals from the Far East and the West. As a result, many Indian animals, such as the elephant and rhinoceros, are similar to those found in southeastern Asia or Africa.

The climate of southeastern Asia is generally warm and humid year round, and tropical rainforests flourish. Many animals live high up in the canopy of the forest where there is more light, water, and food. These rainforests are also home to a huge number of insects. Much of the rainforest has been cleared to make way for farmland and houses, putting animals in danger of extinction. Some of the rarest animals, such as the Javan rhinoceros, survive only in remote parts of the Indonesian islands.

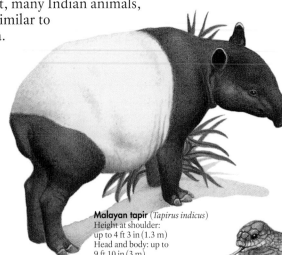

Malayan tapir (*Tapirus indicus*)
Height at shoulder:
up to 4 ft 3 in (1.3 m)
Head and body: up to
9 ft 10 in (3 m)

Handy nose
The Malayan tapir has a long nose that it uses to pull shoots, buds, and fruits from the forest plants. The tapir comes out mainly at night, moving quickly through the forest undergrowth. A good swimmer, it may plunge into the water to escape from enemies.

Hooded poisoner
The king cobra has huge venom glands. A bite can kill an elephant in four hours and a person in just 15–20 minutes. King cobras are normally quiet, but they can be aggressive when defending their eggs. To frighten off an enemy, the king cobra hisses, raises its body, and spreads out the skin around its neck to form a hood.

King cobra
(*Ophiophagus hannah*)
Length: up to 19 ft 2 in (5.9 m)

Asian elephant
(*Elephas maximus*)
Body length: up to
21 ft (6.4 m)
Height at shoulder:
up to 11 ft 1 in (3.4 m)

Atlas moth
(*Attacus atlas*)
Wingspan: up
to 12 in (30 cm)

Wings with eyes
The spots on the wings of the atlas moth may help protect it from enemies—birds, for instance, often peck at the "eyes" on its wings instead of the moth's real eyes. The male has large, feathery antennae, which pick up the scent given off by females that are ready to mate.

Spot the difference
The Asian elephant is similar to its African relative, but has smaller ears, a more humped back, and four nails on each back foot instead of three. Only some of the males have tusks, and these are usually shorter than the tusks of African elephants. Asian elephants live in herds made up of closely related individuals, led by an elderly female.

Armor plating
The Indian rhinoceros looks as if it is wearing a suit of armor because it has thick skin with deep folds at the joints. Its skin protects it from spiky forest plants. The rhinoceros likes to be near water because it often takes baths. It has been hunted for its horn, which is used in Chinese medicine, and is now classed as a vulnerable species.

Indian rhinoceros (*Rhinoceros unicornis*)
Body length: up to 11 ft 4 in (3.5 m)
Height at shoulder: up to 6 ft 7 in (2 m)

ASIAN
ELEPHANT

BLUE
PEAFOWL

INDIAN
RHINOCEROS

Indus

Ganges

Narmada

I N D I A

Godavari

Krishna

A R A B I A N   S E A

KING
COBRA

B A
B E N

KILOMETERS
0   200   400   600   800   1000

0   150   300   450   600
MILES

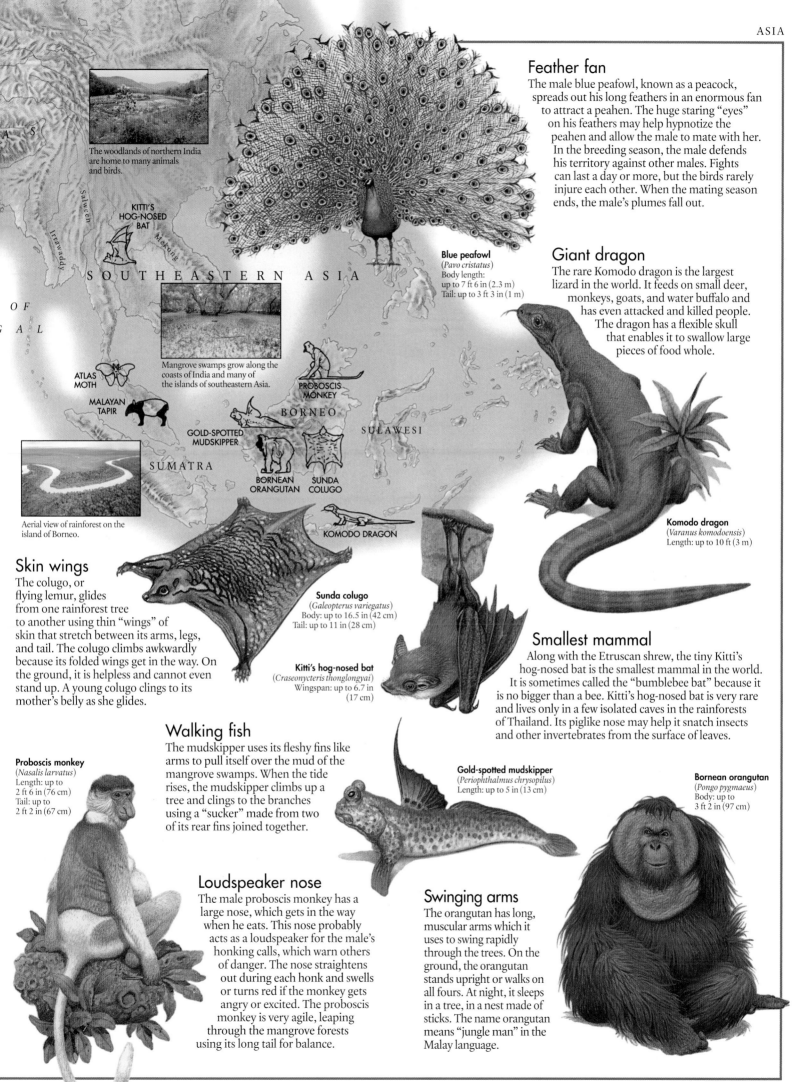

The woodlands of northern India are home to many animals and birds.

KITTI'S HOG-NOSED BAT

SOUTHEASTERN ASIA

Mangrove swamps grow along the coasts of India and many of the islands of southeastern Asia.

ATLAS MOTH

MALAYAN TAPIR

GOLD-SPOTTED MUDSKIPPER

PROBOSCIS MONKEY

BORNEO

SULAWESI

SUMATRA

BORNEAN ORANGUTAN

SUNDA COLUGO

Aerial view of rainforest on the island of Borneo.

KOMODO DRAGON

Feather fan

The male blue peafowl, known as a peacock, spreads out his long feathers in an enormous fan to attract a peahen. The huge staring "eyes" on his feathers may help hypnotize the peahen and allow the male to mate with her. In the breeding season, the male defends his territory against other males. Fights can last a day or more, but the birds rarely injure each other. When the mating season ends, the male's plumes fall out.

Blue peafowl
(*Pavo cristatus*)
Body length:
up to 7 ft 6 in (2.3 m)
Tail: up to 3 ft 3 in (1 m)

Giant dragon

The rare Komodo dragon is the largest lizard in the world. It feeds on small deer, monkeys, goats, and water buffalo and has even attacked and killed people. The dragon has a flexible skull that enables it to swallow large pieces of food whole.

Komodo dragon
(*Varanus komodoensis*)
Length: up to 10 ft (3 m)

Skin wings

The colugo, or flying lemur, glides from one rainforest tree to another using thin "wings" of skin that stretch between its arms, legs, and tail. The colugo climbs awkwardly because its folded wings get in the way. On the ground, it is helpless and cannot even stand up. A young colugo clings to its mother's belly as she glides.

Sunda colugo
(*Galeopterus variegatus*)
Body: up to 16.5 in (42 cm)
Tail: up to 11 in (28 cm)

Kitti's hog-nosed bat
(*Craseonycteris thonglongyai*)
Wingspan: up to 6.7 in
(17 cm)

Smallest mammal

Along with the Etruscan shrew, the tiny Kitti's hog-nosed bat is the smallest mammal in the world. It is sometimes called the "bumblebee bat" because it is no bigger than a bee. Kitti's hog-nosed bat is very rare and lives only in a few isolated caves in the rainforests of Thailand. Its piglike nose may help it snatch insects and other invertebrates from the surface of leaves.

Walking fish

The mudskipper uses its fleshy fins like arms to pull itself over the mud of the mangrove swamps. When the tide rises, the mudskipper climbs up a tree and clings to the branches using a "sucker" made from two of its rear fins joined together.

Proboscis monkey
(*Nasalis larvatus*)
Length: up to
2 ft 6 in (76 cm)
Tail: up to
2 ft 2 in (67 cm)

Gold-spotted mudskipper
(*Periophthalmus chrysopilus*)
Length: up to 5 in (13 cm)

Bornean orangutan
(*Pongo pygmaeus*)
Body: up to
3 ft 2 in (97 cm)

Loudspeaker nose

The male proboscis monkey has a large nose, which gets in the way when he eats. This nose probably acts as a loudspeaker for the male's honking calls, which warn others of danger. The nose straightens out during each honk and swells or turns red if the monkey gets angry or excited. The proboscis monkey is very agile, leaping through the mangrove forests using its long tail for balance.

Swinging arms

The orangutan has long, muscular arms which it uses to swing rapidly through the trees. On the ground, the orangutan stands upright or walks on all fours. At night, it sleeps in a tree, in a nest made of sticks. The name orangutan means "jungle man" in the Malay language.

The Outback

THE DRY, DESERTLIKE PLAINS of the Australian outback cover more than two-thirds of the continent. Much of the region receives less than 10 in (250 mm) of rainfall a year. Although the rains may come at any time of the year, there are often long periods of drought, which are difficult to survive. Many of the animals avoid the heat of the day by staying in their burrows, since it is cooler and damper underground. Some small animals sleep underground through the hottest summer months. This is called aestivation. Many animals can also survive with little or no water. Their bodies are adapted to store water from their food and to lose very little water in their urine.

Mallee fowl
(*Leipoa ocellata*)
Length: up to
2 ft (60 cm)

Compost nest
The male mallee fowl builds a huge mound of compost in which the female lays her eggs. The heat given off by the rotting compost keeps the eggs warm. When the chicks hatch, they push their way up to the surface.

Short-beaked echidna
(*Tachyglossus aculeatus*)
Length: up to 17.8 in (45 cm)
Spines: up to 2 in (6 cm)

Spiny coat
The echidna's long, sharp spines help protect it from enemies. If it is attacked, it rolls itself into a ball or digs straight down into the soil. This hides its soft face and spineless underparts.

Frilled lizard
(*Chlamydosaurus kingii*)
Length including tail:
up to 3 ft (90 cm)

Frightening frill
When a frilled lizard is attacked, it opens out the flap of skin around its neck to make it bigger and more dangerous-looking. It rises up and runs on its hind legs. Its bright mouth also helps it scare away enemies.

Greater bilby
(*Macrotis lagotis*)
Length including tail:
up to 33 in (84 cm)

Uluru, in central Australia, is the world's largest freestanding rock.

A U S T R A L

GREATER
BILBY

GREAT SANDY DESERT

CENTRALIAN
BLUE-TONGUED
SKINK

EMU

PERENTIE

GIBSON
DESERT

DINGO

BRUSH-TAILED
MULGARA

Lake
Amadeus

MALLEE FOWL

CENTRAL DESERT
MARSUPIAL
MOLE

THORNY
DEVIL

SHORT-BEAKED
ECHIDNA

Lake Eyre

GREAT VICTORIA
DESERT

SOUTHERN HAIRY-
NOSED WOMBAT

Lake Torrens

Lake
Gairdner

NULLARBOR PLAIN

GREAT AUSTRALIAN BIGHT

I N D I A N   O C E A N

Bottle trees survive in dry areas by storing water under their bark.

Deep digger
The greater bilby uses its strong claws to dig burrows up to 6 ft (2 m) deep. The female's pouch opens under her tail; this keeps dirt off her baby. To escape the heat of day, bilbies stay in their burrows.

Emu (*Dromaius novaehollandiae*)
Height: up to 6 ft 3 in (1.9 m)

High-speed runner
Emus cannot fly, but they have strong legs and massive feet and can run at up to 30 mph (48 kph). The emu is the second largest bird in the world. It eats grass, berries, fruit, and insects but has been known to swallow marbles, nails, and even coins.

Perentie
(*Varanus giganteus*)
Length including tail:
up to 8 ft 3 in (2.5 m)

Huge lizard
The perentie is one of the world's largest lizards. With powerful jaws, huge claws, and sharp, curved teeth, it can catch snakes, rabbits, birds, and even small kangaroos. It whips its heavy tail sideways to defend itself.

Long jumper

The red kangaroo bounds along on its enormous back legs, using its strong tail to help it balance. A big male kangaroo can clear more than 30 ft (9 m) in one leap. Usually only the male has red fur. The female is blue-gray in color.

Red kangaroo
(*Osphranter rufus*)
Height: up to
4 ft 7 in (1.4 m)
Tail: up to 3 ft 3 in
(1 m)

Tunneling mole

The marsupial mole uses its long claws to dig tunnels in soft sand dunes. Its body is a smooth, streamlined shape and it pushes easily through the sand. The mole spends all of its life underground in dark tunnels, so it has no eyes.

Central desert marsupial mole
(*Notoryctes typhlops*)
Length: up to
5.5 in (14 cm)

Brush-tailed mulgara
(*Dasycercus blythi*)
Length including tail:
up to 10 in (26.5 cm)

Big eater

The mulgara eats up to 25 percent of its own weight in meat every day, eating mice, birds, and small lizards. During the day, the mulgara stays in its burrow, out of the heat.

Centralian blue-tongued skink
(*Tiliqua multifasciata*)
Length: up to 17.7 in
(45 cm)

Scary tongue

When a blue-tongued skink is frightened, it puts out its bright blue tongue and makes a hissing sound. Although this display may help scare off attackers, the skink is really quite harmless.

CORAL SEA

FRILLED LIZARD
I A

GREAT DIVIDING RANGE

WATER-HOLDING FROG

RED KANGAROO

Darling

Murray

PACIFIC OCEAN

Thorny devil
(*Moloch horridus*)
Length including tail: up to 7.8 in (20 cm)

Termite nests are common in the outback and may be up to 20 ft (6 m) high.

KILOMETERS
0   200   400   600
0   200   400
MILES

BASS STRAIT

TASMANIA

Desert devil

The thorny devil is a type of lizard covered in hard spines to protect it from attack. It gets liquid from dew that collects on its skin at night. The dew runs along thousands of tiny grooves on the lizard's skin into its mouth.

Wild dog

Dingos are descended from domesticated dogs that people brought to Australia about 4,000 years ago, but they have become wild again. Dingos yelp or howl instead of barking.

Dingo (*Canis lupis dingo*)
Height at shoulder: up to
20 in (50 cm)
Length: up to 3 ft 3 in (1 m)

Huge burrow

The Southern hairy-nosed wombat avoids the heat of the day by staying in a deep burrow, which can be up to 100 ft (30 m) long. Feeding mainly on grass, it can go without water for months at a time.

Southern hairy-nosed wombat
(*Lasiorhinus latifrons*)
Body length:
up to 3 ft 8 in
(111 cm)

Water tank

The water-holding frog stores water in its bladder. A large frog can hold half its own weight in water. It also produces an outer layer of skin that forms a watery cocoon around its body, helping it survive in droughts.

Water-holding frog
(*Cyclorana platycephalus*)
Length: up to 2 in (6 cm)

Rainforests and Woods

THE LUSH TROPICAL RAINFORESTS of northeastern Australia are very different from the dry interior of the continent. Hot and damp, they provide a home for an unusual variety of animals, from tree kangaroos to spectacular birds of paradise. Similar wildlife is found in the misty mountain forests of New Guinea, an island about 1,400 miles (2,200 km) long, which lies off northern Australia. In the southwest and southeast of Australia there are cooler, drier eucalyptus woods, where rain falls mainly during the winter months. Many birds nest there in the winter and early spring. The trees and shrubs are a rich source of nectar and pollen for animals such as parrots and bats.

Western spinebill
(*Acanthorhynchus superciliosus*)
Length: up to 6 in (15.5 cm)

Nectar eater

The western spinebill uses its long, curved bill to probe for nectar in flowers. Its tongue has a brush at the tip, which the bird uses to lap up nectar.

Powerful poison

The taipan is one of the most venomous snakes in the world. One taipan can contain enough venom (poison) to kill 125,000 mice, and its fangs are 0.5 in (1 cm) long. Although the taipan is normally timid, it becomes very fierce when threatened.

Sydney funnel-web spider
(*Atrax robustus*)
Length: up to 1.3 in (3.5 cm)

Taipan
(*Oxyuranus scutellatus*)
Length: up to 10 ft 10 in (3.3 m)

QUEEN ALEXANDRA'S BIRDWING BUTTERFLY

N E W

Dense rainforest vegetation in eastern New Guinea.

Silky killer

The funnel-web spider lives in a burrow with an entrance shaped like a funnel. It lines the burrow with a silky web, which is extremely sticky. At night, the spider emerges to seize small animals, insects, and other prey. It injects venom into its victims and is one of the few spiders that can kill people.

Non-slip soles

The tree kangaroo has strong, wide paws with rough pads and sharp claws to help it climb in the trees. Its long tail helps the kangaroo balance on branches.

Goodfellow's tree kangaroo
(*Dendrolagus goodfellowi*)
Body length: up to 2 ft 9 in (84.5 cm)
Tail: up to 2 ft 9 in (85.5 cm)

BLUE-WINGED KOOKABURRA

TANAMI DESERT

Many palm trees grow on Australia's coastal plain.

Dancing display

The rainbow lorikeet hops and preens to warn other lorikeets to keep out of its territory. The male uses similar moves to win a female during courtship.

Rainbow lorikeet
(*Trichoglossus moluccanus*)
Length: up to 12 in (30 cm)

INDIAN OCEAN

A U S T R A L

Ashburton

Gascoyne

Lake Amadeus

SIMPSON DESERT

Δ Ayers Rock

NUMBAT

Rainforest grows on the northern mountains of the Great Dividing Range.

Lake Eyre

Lake Torrens

Lake Gairdner

Furry parachute

The sugar glider has webs of skin between its front and back legs, which it stretches out like a parachute to slow down as it glides between trees. It can cover distances of more than 164 ft (50 m) in one glide. The sugar glider feeds on insects, nectar, fruit, and the sweet, sugary sap of the eucalyptus tree.

HONEY POSSUM

GREAT AUSTRALIAN BIGHT

FLINDERS RANGES

WESTERN SPINEBILL

Sugar glider
(*Petaurus breviceps*)
Body length: up to 8 in (21 cm)
Tail: up to 8 in (21 cm)

KILOMETERS
0   200   400   600
0   200   400
MILES

Leafy diet

The koala has a very narrow diet—it eats only the leaves of certain eucalyptus trees. It stores the leaves in its cheek pouches and has an extra-long intestine to help digest them. The koala gets most of its moisture from its food and rarely drinks water—in fact, its name comes from an Aboriginal word meaning "no drink." The koala can curl its fingers and toes around branches to get a good grip and has claws like knives.

Koala
(*Phascolarctos cinerenus*)
Length: up to 2 ft 8 in (82 cm)

Raggiana bird of paradise
(*Paradisaea raggiana*)
Body length with tail wires:
up to 28 in (68 cm)

Biggest butterfly

The Queen Alexandra's birdwing butterfly is the world's largest butterfly. It is now very rare, due to overcollecting and the destruction of the rainforests. This butterfly usually flies high above the ground, where the sun filters through the trees.

Queen Alexandra's birdwing butterfly
(*Ornithoptera alexandrae*)
Wingspan: up to 9.8 in (25 cm)

Northern leaf-tailed gecko
(*Saltuarius cornutus*)
Length: up to 9.8 in (25 cm)

Fantastic feathers

The male Raggiana bird of paradise shows off his spectacular feathers to compete against other males and win a female. In contrast, the feathers of the female bird are plain.

Invisible animal

During the daytime, the leaf-tailed gecko is perfectly camouflaged against the mossy tree trunks in the rainforests. Its flattened shape also means it casts few shadows.

Flower feeder

The honey possum uses its long snout to probe into flowers for pollen, nectar, and insects. It has a long, thin tongue tipped with bristles for soaking up its food.

Honey possum (*Tarsipes rostratus*)
Body length: up to 3.5 in (9 cm)

Toothy mammal

The numbat has a long tongue, which it uses to lick up termites and ants. It has about 50 teeth—among the most of any land mammal.

Numbat
(*Myrmecobius fasciatus*)
Body length: up to
11.4 in (29 cm)
Tail: up to 8 in (20.3 cm)

Blue-winged kookaburra
(*Dacelo leachii*)
Length: up to
16 in (41 cm)

Alarm clock bird

The kookaburra's noisy cackles, screeches, and barks tell others to keep out of its territory. Kookaburras often call early in the morning, waking people up.

GUINEA

RAGGIANA BIRD OF PARADISE

GOODFELLOW'S TREE KANGAROO

SUGAR GLIDER

TAIPAN

NORTHERN LEAF-TAILED GECKO

KOALA

I A

PACIFIC OCEAN

GREAT DIVIDING RANGE

Darling

RAINBOW LORIKEET

Murray

SYDNEY FUNNEL-WEB SPIDER

The Barrier Reef

THE BIGGEST coral reef in the world is the Great Barrier Reef, which stretches nearly 1,250 miles (2,000 km) along the northeastern coast of Australia. Over millions of years, the limestone skeletons of tiny animals called corals build up on top of one another to make a reef. Reefs form only in warm, salty waters that are shallow enough for sunlight to reach the corals. Many plants and animals can feed and grow on a reef. The Great Barrier Reef is home to a large variety of creatures, including more than 1,500 species of fish, 1,400 species of coral, and many types of sponges.

Stinging tentacles

This orange cup coral looks like a plant, but it is really an animal. It uses stinging cells on its tentacles to catch tiny living things floating past in the water.

Orange cup coral (*Tubastraea coccinea*)
Diameter of each coral: up to 0.43 in (11 mm)

Reef wrecker

The crown-of-thorns starfish turns its stomach inside out and pours digestive juices over living coral to eat it, leaving only the coral's skeleton behind. One starfish can eat up to 280 sq in (1,800 sq cm) of coral in a day. These creatures have caused much damage to the Great Barrier Reef.

Crown-of-thorns starfish
(*Acanthaster planci*)
Diameter: up to
2 ft 7 in (80 cm)

Hinged shell

The giant clam weighs up to 550 lbs (250 kg). Its shell is in two parts, joined by a hinge. The clam usually opens its shell so that it can feed, but can quickly close the shell in the face of danger. Clams can live for hundreds of years.

Giant clam (*Tridacna*)
Width of shell: up to
4 ft 6 in (1.4 m)

Attractive patterns

The bright colors and patterns of butterflyfishes help them recognize each other and attract mates. Each kind of butterflyfish has its own place on the reef and feeds on a different food.

Threadfin butterflyfish
(*Chaetodon auriga*)
Length: up to 9 in (23 cm)

Free food

The cleaner wrasse gets food from other fish on the reef. It eats their parasites (animals that live on and in their bodies) and their dead scales. It stops larger fish from eating it by dancing to signal that it is a friend.

Blue-streaked cleaner wrasse
(*Labroides dimidiatus*)
Length: up to 5.5 in (14 cm)

Special friends

Sea anemones have venomous tentacles that kill the small fish they eat. The clownfish is not harmed by this poison and lives among the tentacles, where it is safe from enemies. In return, the fish helps feed the anemone with waste and leftovers.

CAPE
YORK
PENINSULA

GREAT BARRIER REEF
MARINE PARK

GIANT
CLAM

BLUE-
STREAKED
CLEANER
WRASSE

CROWN-OF-
THORNS
STARFISH

GREAT BARRIER REEF

Underwater view of sea lilies, corals, and sponges.

A U S T R A L I A

When coral is not covered by sea water, it loses its bright colors.

ORANGE
CLOWNFISH AND
GIANT CARPET
ANEMONE

THREADFIN
BUTTERFLYFISH

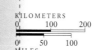

ORANGE
CUP CORAL

The Great Barrier Reef is so big that it can be seen from the Moon.

KILOMETERS
0   100   200

0   50   100
MILES

Orange clownfish
(*Amphiprion percula*)
Length: up to 4 in (11 cm)

Giant carpet anemone
(*Stichodactyla gigantea*)
Width: up to 2 ft 7 in (80 cm)

GREAT BARRIER REEF
MARINE PARK

Tasmania

THE ISLAND OF TASMANIA was once part of mainland Australia, but it is now separated from southeastern Australia by the Bass Strait. Tasmania has a cool, wet climate. The western part of the island contains rainforest that is home to many animals. Tasmania's isolation has allowed some animals to develop into unusual forms or separate species. Species have been threatened by introduced species, such as rabbits, although not as badly as those in mainland Australia. Clearing forest for logging and mining is the biggest issue.

Reluctant flier

The ground parrot spends most of its time on the ground. It can fly, but rarely goes more than 650 ft (200 m) before landing.

Ground parrot
(*Pezoporus wallicus*)
Length: up to 12 in (30 cm)

Forest demon

The Tasmanian devil's name comes from its black coloring and its eerie, whining snarl. It has strong jaws and teeth that can crush bones. It eats all of its prey—bones, fur, skin, or feathers—leaving nothing behind.

KING ISLAND

BASS STRAIT

Big mouth

The quoll is a pouched mammal that comes out mainly at night to hunt. Its jaws can open wide to show its pointed teeth. The quoll has sharp claws and ridged pads on its back feet for climbing.

Spotted-tailed quoll
(*Dasyurus maculatus*)
Body length: up to 2 ft 6 in (76 cm)

Bony bill

The platypus is an unusual mammal because it lays eggs. Its bill is made of a bone frame covered with skin. When swimming underwater, the platypus shuts its ears and eyes and uses its sensitive bill to probe for food. Most dives last less than a minute.

Tasmanian devil
(*Sarcophilus harrisi*)
Body length: up to 2 ft 1 in (65 cm)

INDIAN OCEAN

PLATYPUS

Lake Mackintosh

Great Lake

Thick vegetation covers the banks of the Franklin River in southwestern Tasmania.

Many of the mountainous areas of Tasmania are covered by forest.

TASMAN SEA

T A S M A N I A

SPOTTED-TAILED QUOLL

THYLACINE

RUFOUS-BELLIED PADEMELON

TASMANIAN DEVIL

Lake Gordon

GROUND PARROT

Rare wolf

The thylacine or Tasmanian wolf is declared extinct, although there have been unverified sightings. It was a pouched mammal with a thick tail like a kangaroo's, but had doglike feet and teeth. It also whined, barked, and growled like a dog.

Thylacine
(*Thylacinus cynocephalus*)
Body length: up to 4 ft (1.2 m)
Tail: up to 2 ft (61 cm)

Rufous-bellied pademelon
(*Thylogale billardierii*)
Length: up to 2 ft (63 cm)
Tail: up to 16.5 in (42 cm)

KILOMETERS
0   20   40   60
0   10   20   30
MILES

Platypus
(*Ornithorhynchus anatinus*)
Length including tail: up to 25 in (63 cm)
Bill: up to 2.4 in (6 cm)

Tunneling wallaby

The rufous-bellied pademelon is a type of kangaroo that takes shelter in the undergrowth. If a pademelon is alarmed, it may thump the ground with its back legs to warn others of approaching danger.

New Zealand

THE ISLANDS of New Zealand lie about 1,000 miles (1,600 km) east of Australia. New Zealand has a cool, wet climate in which forests and grasslands flourish. New Zealand split off from the other landmasses about 80 million years ago, before mammals became a major animal group. As a result, there are only two land mammals native to the country, both of them bats. Birds have been able to take advantage of the lack of mammals in New Zealand, and often live in habitats normally used by mammals elsewhere.

Northern brown kiwi
(*Apteryx mantelli*)
Height: up to 25.5 in (65 cm)
Bill: up to 1 ft (30 cm)

Furry feathers
The brown kiwi is a flightless bird. It is covered in long feathers that look like fur. The kiwi hunts at night for worms and insects. It finds its prey with its acute hearing and the nostrils on the tip of its sensitive bill.

Crawling bat
The rare New Zealand short-tailed bat is good at moving around on the ground and can run fast on all fours, even up steep slopes.

Kea
(*Nestor notabilis*)
Length: up to 19 in (48 cm)

Hamilton's frog
Leiopelma hamiltoni
Length: up to 2 in (5 cm)

New Zealand lesser short-tailed bat
(*Mystacina tuberculata*)
Wingspan: up to 12 in (30 cm)

Ancient frog
Frogs like the rare Hamilton's frog lived 150 million years ago. This frog has no eardrums or vocal sac. It develops into a froglet while it is inside the egg.

Snow parrot
The kea is an unusual parrot that lives in the snowy Southern Alps. It uses its beak to dig up roots and shoots under the snow, but it also eats meat. It has been known to eat hikers' boots and to tear up campers' tents.

The Southern Alps contain many lakes, which were carved out by glaciers during the Ice Age.

KILOMETERS
0   50   100   150

0   25   50   75   100
MILES

BAY OF PLENTY

N O R T H
I S L A N D

Lake Taupo

NORTHERN BROWN KIWI

HAWKE BAY

Land on the slopes of the eastern hills on the North Island is used for grazing sheep and dairy cattle.

TUATARA

RAUKUMARA RANGE

HAMILTON'S FROG

TASMAN MTS

TASMAN BAY

COOK STRAIT

TARARUA RANGE

TASMAN SEA

SOUTHERN ALPS

S O U T H   I S L A N D

CANTERBURY PLAINS

PACIFIC OCEAN

KEA

NEW ZEALAND LESSER SHORT-TAILED BAT

Evergreen trees and tree ferns are the most common plants in New Zealand's forests.

Flightless parrot
The kakapo, or owl parrot, is the world's only flightless parrot. It only uses its short wings to glide down from trees, and it can run very fast. It comes out at night to hunt for berries, roots, leaves, and lizards.

Kakapo
(*Strigops habroptila*)
Length: up to 2 ft 1 in (64 cm)

KAKAPO

STEWART ISLAND

Tuatara
(*Sphenodon punctatus*)
Length: up to 2 ft 6 in (76 cm)

Special survivor
The tuatara is related to a group of reptiles that lived during the age of the dinosaurs. The male can raise the spines along his back to scare off other animals. Tuataras can live for 120 years.

Antarctica

ANTARCTICA IS THE WORLD'S coldest and most isolated continent. The average temperature at the South Pole is –56°F (–49°C). In the winter months, it is dark all the time and temperatures as low as –128.6°F (–89.2°C) have been recorded. Antarctica is also one of the windiest places on Earth—the wind speed can reach 200 mph (322 kph). A permanent cap of ice covers most of the continent. In some places, this ice is over 2.5 miles (4 km) thick. In these harsh conditions only a few tiny insects and spiders manage to survive on the land, but the seas are rich in food and support huge numbers of animals.

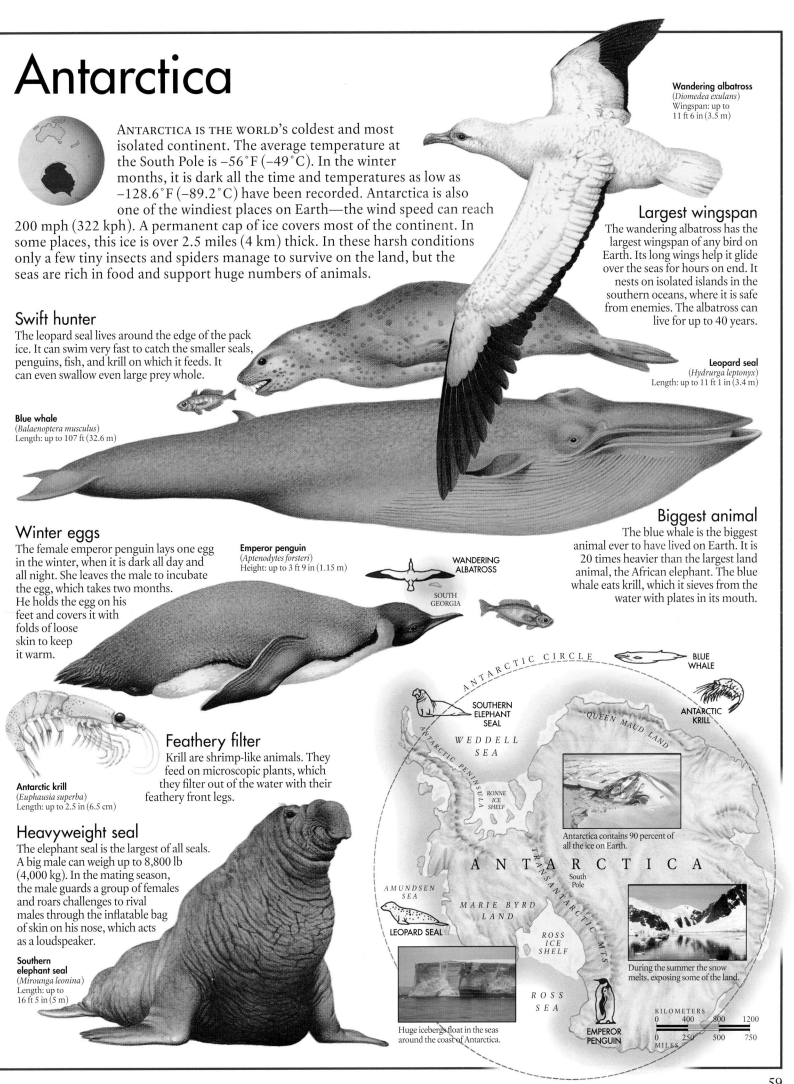

Wandering albatross
(*Diomedea exulans*)
Wingspan: up to
11 ft 6 in (3.5 m)

Swift hunter
The leopard seal lives around the edge of the pack ice. It can swim very fast to catch the smaller seals, penguins, fish, and krill on which it feeds. It can even swallow even large prey whole.

Largest wingspan
The wandering albatross has the largest wingspan of any bird on Earth. Its long wings help it glide over the seas for hours on end. It nests on isolated islands in the southern oceans, where it is safe from enemies. The albatross can live for up to 40 years.

Leopard seal
(*Hydrurga leptonyx*)
Length: up to 11 ft 1 in (3.4 m)

Blue whale
(*Balaenoptera musculus*)
Length: up to 107 ft (32.6 m)

Winter eggs
The female emperor penguin lays one egg in the winter, when it is dark all day and all night. She leaves the male to incubate the egg, which takes two months. He holds the egg on his feet and covers it with folds of loose skin to keep it warm.

Emperor penguin
(*Aptenodytes forsteri*)
Height: up to 3 ft 9 in (1.15 m)

Biggest animal
The blue whale is the biggest animal ever to have lived on Earth. It is 20 times heavier than the largest land animal, the African elephant. The blue whale eats krill, which it sieves from the water with plates in its mouth.

Feathery filter
Krill are shrimp-like animals. They feed on microscopic plants, which they filter out of the water with their feathery front legs.

Antarctic krill
(*Euphausia superba*)
Length: up to 2.5 in (6.5 cm)

Heavyweight seal
The elephant seal is the largest of all seals. A big male can weigh up to 8,800 lb (4,000 kg). In the mating season, the male guards a group of females and roars challenges to rival males through the inflatable bag of skin on his nose, which acts as a loudspeaker.

Southern elephant seal
(*Mirounga leonina*)
Length: up to
16 ft 5 in (5 m)

WANDERING ALBATROSS

SOUTH GEORGIA

ANTARCTIC CIRCLE

BLUE WHALE

SOUTHERN ELEPHANT SEAL

ANTARCTIC KRILL

QUEEN MAUD LAND

WEDDELL SEA

ANTARCTIC PENINSULA

RONNE ICE SHELF

Antarctica contains 90 percent of all the ice on Earth.

AMUNDSEN SEA

MARIE BYRD LAND

ANTARCTICA

TRANSANTARCTIC MTS

South Pole

LEOPARD SEAL

ROSS ICE SHELF

ROSS SEA

During the summer the snow melts, exposing some of the land.

Huge icebergs float in the seas around the coast of Antarctica.

EMPEROR PENGUIN

KILOMETERS
0   400   800   1200

0   250   500   750
MILES

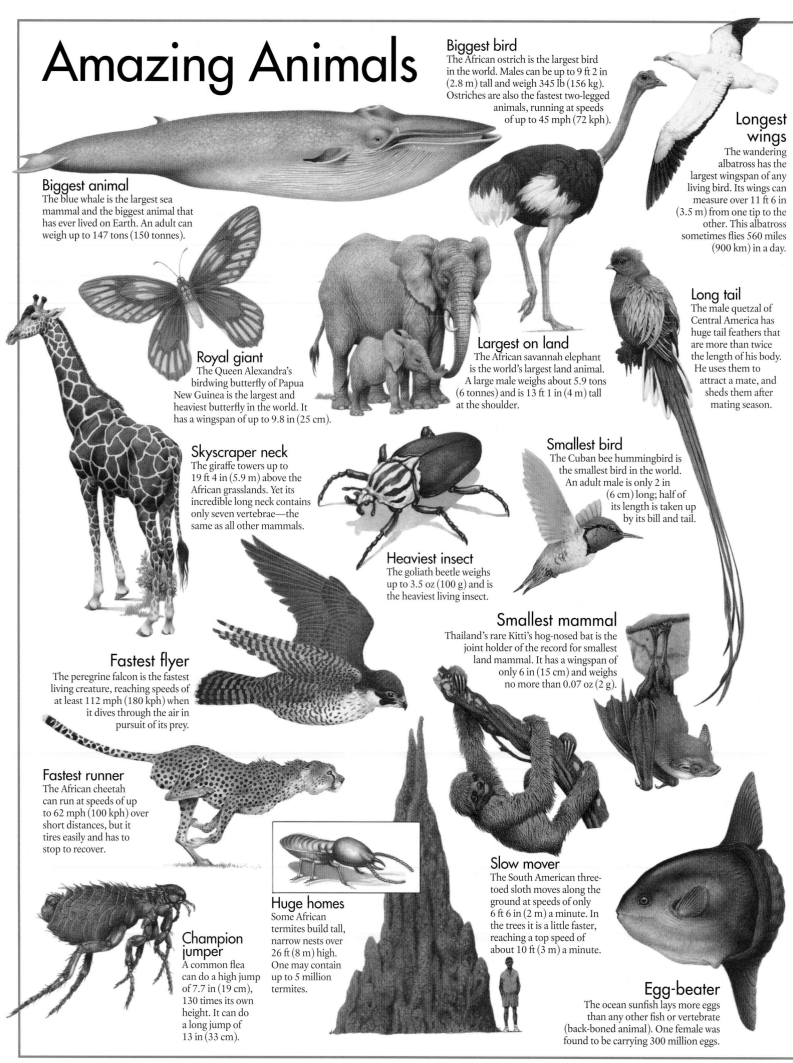

Amazing Animals

Biggest bird
The African ostrich is the largest bird in the world. Males can be up to 9 ft 2 in (2.8 m) tall and weigh 345 lb (156 kg). Ostriches are also the fastest two-legged animals, running at speeds of up to 45 mph (72 kph).

Longest wings
The wandering albatross has the largest wingspan of any living bird. Its wings can measure over 11 ft 6 in (3.5 m) from one tip to the other. This albatross sometimes flies 560 miles (900 km) in a day.

Biggest animal
The blue whale is the largest sea mammal and the biggest animal that has ever lived on Earth. An adult can weigh up to 147 tons (150 tonnes).

Long tail
The male quetzal of Central America has huge tail feathers that are more than twice the length of his body. He uses them to attract a mate, and sheds them after mating season.

Royal giant
The Queen Alexandra's birdwing butterfly of Papua New Guinea is the largest and heaviest butterfly in the world. It has a wingspan of up to 9.8 in (25 cm).

Largest on land
The African savannah elephant is the world's largest land animal. A large male weighs about 5.9 tons (6 tonnes) and is 13 ft 1 in (4 m) tall at the shoulder.

Skyscraper neck
The giraffe towers up to 19 ft 4 in (5.9 m) above the African grasslands. Yet its incredible long neck contains only seven vertebrae—the same as all other mammals.

Smallest bird
The Cuban bee hummingbird is the smallest bird in the world. An adult male is only 2 in (6 cm) long; half of its length is taken up by its bill and tail.

Heaviest insect
The goliath beetle weighs up to 3.5 oz (100 g) and is the heaviest living insect.

Smallest mammal
Thailand's rare Kitti's hog-nosed bat is the joint holder of the record for smallest land mammal. It has a wingspan of only 6 in (15 cm) and weighs no more than 0.07 oz (2 g).

Fastest flyer
The peregrine falcon is the fastest living creature, reaching speeds of at least 112 mph (180 kph) when it dives through the air in pursuit of its prey.

Fastest runner
The African cheetah can run at speeds of up to 62 mph (100 kph) over short distances, but it tires easily and has to stop to recover.

Slow mover
The South American three-toed sloth moves along the ground at speeds of only 6 ft 6 in (2 m) a minute. In the trees it is a little faster, reaching a top speed of about 10 ft (3 m) a minute.

Champion jumper
A common flea can do a high jump of 7.7 in (19 cm), 130 times its own height. It can do a long jump of 13 in (33 cm).

Huge homes
Some African termites build tall, narrow nests over 26 ft (8 m) high. One may contain up to 5 million termites.

Egg-beater
The ocean sunfish lays more eggs than any other fish or vertebrate (back-boned animal). One female was found to be carrying 300 million eggs.

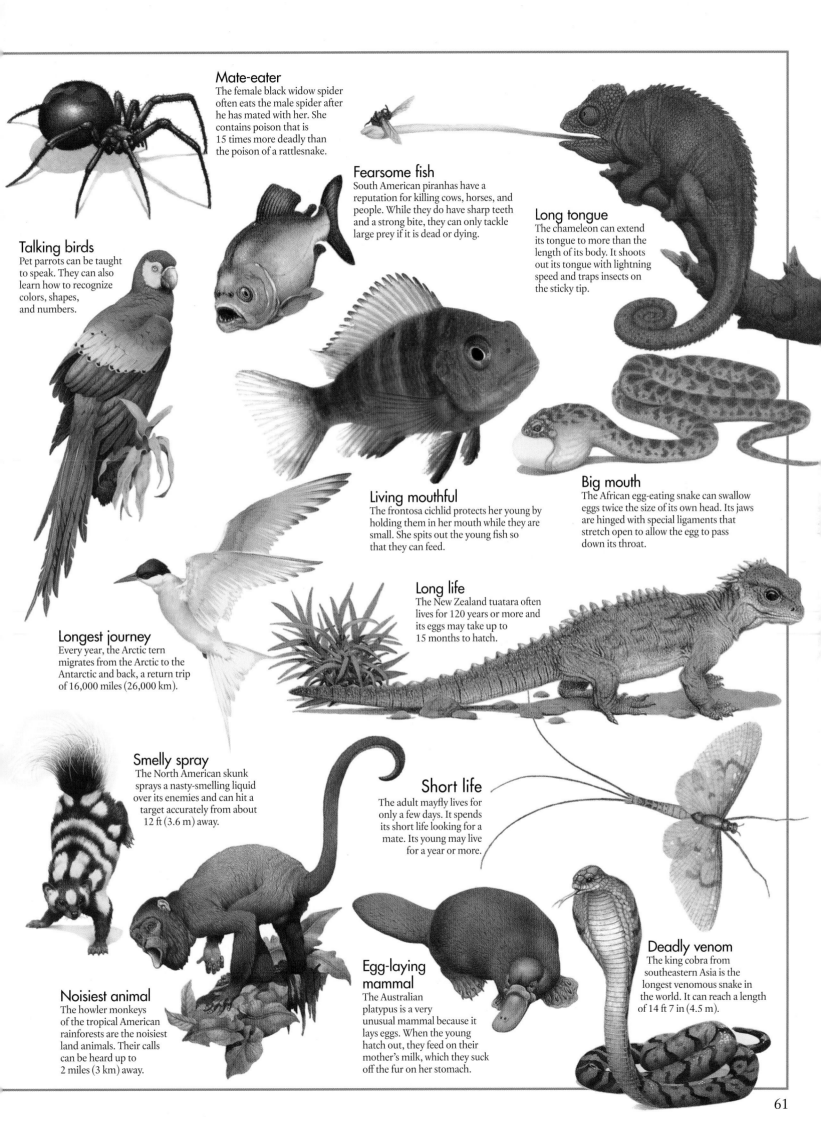

Mate-eater
The female black widow spider often eats the male spider after he has mated with her. She contains poison that is 15 times more deadly than the poison of a rattlesnake.

Fearsome fish
South American piranhas have a reputation for killing cows, horses, and people. While they do have sharp teeth and a strong bite, they can only tackle large prey if it is dead or dying.

Long tongue
The chameleon can extend its tongue to more than the length of its body. It shoots out its tongue with lightning speed and traps insects on the sticky tip.

Talking birds
Pet parrots can be taught to speak. They can also learn how to recognize colors, shapes, and numbers.

Living mouthful
The frontosa cichlid protects her young by holding them in her mouth while they are small. She spits out the young fish so that they can feed.

Big mouth
The African egg-eating snake can swallow eggs twice the size of its own head. Its jaws are hinged with special ligaments that stretch open to allow the egg to pass down its throat.

Long life
The New Zealand tuatara often lives for 120 years or more and its eggs may take up to 15 months to hatch.

Longest journey
Every year, the Arctic tern migrates from the Arctic to the Antarctic and back, a return trip of 16,000 miles (26,000 km).

Smelly spray
The North American skunk sprays a nasty-smelling liquid over its enemies and can hit a target accurately from about 12 ft (3.6 m) away.

Short life
The adult mayfly lives for only a few days. It spends its short life looking for a mate. Its young may live for a year or more.

Noisiest animal
The howler monkeys of the tropical American rainforests are the noisiest land animals. Their calls can be heard up to 2 miles (3 km) away.

Egg-laying mammal
The Australian platypus is a very unusual mammal because it lays eggs. When the young hatch out, they feed on their mother's milk, which they suck off the fur on her stomach.

Deadly venom
The king cobra from southeastern Asia is the longest venomous snake in the world. It can reach a length of 14 ft 7 in (4.5 m).

61

Animals in Danger

WHOOPING CRANE

LOGGERHEAD TURTLE

NORTH AMERICA

CALIFORNIA CONDOR

AGASSIZ'S DESERT TORTOISE

WEST INDIAN MANATEE

ST. VINCENT AMAZON

CUBAN SOLENODON

MOUNTAIN TAPIR

GIANT TORTOISE

BLACK SPIDER MONKEY

GIANT OTTER

SOUTH AMERICA

CHILEAN CHINCHILLA

GOLDEN LION TAMARIN

GIANT ANTEATER

DARWIN'S FROG

IBERIAN LYNX

ADDAX

PACIFIC OCEAN

ATLANTIC OCEAN

IMAGINE A WORLD WITHOUT elephants, rhinos, and giant pandas. It would be tragic if these creatures vanished forever. Animals make our world a more beautiful and interesting place to live in. We also depend on some animals for food and medicines, and for helping us grow crops and carry heavy loads.

Since life began on Earth about 4,280 million years ago, as many as 500 million species of plants and animals may have lived on our planet. Over millions of years, some of these plants and animals died out because of changes in the environment, and new species developed that were better suited to the changed conditions. This slow process of change is called evolution. Some species survive for millions of years without evolving much at all. Others die out after a few thousand years.

Nowadays, species are becoming extinct much faster than they would naturally because people hunt them or destroy their habitats. This upsets the delicate balance of life on the planet. You can find out more about some of the things that threaten animals across the bottom of these two pages. Three-quarters of the extinctions that happened in the last 300 years were caused by people. Currently, scientists believe that thousands of species of plants and animals are endangered—maybe as many as 20 percent—and by the end of this century, we could lose 50 percent. The IUCN (International Union for Conservation of Nature) has assessed more than 93,500 animal species for how endangered they are. Of these, almost 26,200 species are now at risk of extinction.

HABITAT DESTRUCTION

Iberian lynx

The main threat to the survival of endangered animals comes from people destroying their habitat. Each species of animal is suited to its particular surroundings and cannot usually move elsewhere if this habitat is destroyed. People have cut down forests for their timber or to make way for farms, mines, roads, and cities, endangering animals such as the Iberian lynx or gorilla that once lived there. Without trees, the soil may be washed away by the rain or blown away by the wind, creating land which is of no use to people or animals. Marshlands and swamps are drained to provide more space for the rapidly increasing human population. Hedges are dug up to make fields where farm machines can work more easily. Land may also be flooded to make reservoirs that supply cities with water or to produce electricity inside dams. In some countries, large areas have been destroyed to extract minerals or fuel from the ground.

There are probably only about 300 mountain gorillas left in central Africa. They are threatened by the destruction of their habitat.

Every minute, an area of rainforest the size of 80 hockey pitches is destroyed. At this rate, all the rainforests could disappear within the next 50 years.

HUNTING AND COLLECTING

Rhetenor blue morpho

Many animals are hunted for sport or for valuable parts of their bodies. Animals with beautiful skins, such as leopards and cheetahs, are killed so that their skins can be made into coats, shoes, or bags. Most of this killing is illegal, but as long as people are willing to pay for the goods, the trade will go on. Often animals are killed for one part of their body, such as their horns or tusks, and the rest of the body is left to rot. Rhinos, for example, are killed for their horns, which can be made into dagger handles.

In the past, many animals were taken from the wild to become part of scientific collections. Nowadays, scientists are more interested in preserving wild animals in their natural habitats. But some are still collected for medical research, or to be sold as pets. Rare butterflies, such as the rhetenor blue morpho, are endangered by butterfly collectors, while many rare birds are put at greater risk of extinction by people who collect their eggs.

Fur coats are a luxury that we can survive without, and we can now make artificial fur coats which look just like the real thing, rather than taking fur from animals.

Tiger numbers have declined, owing to poaching and destruction of their forest habitat. An illegal trade in the skin, bones, and meat continues today.

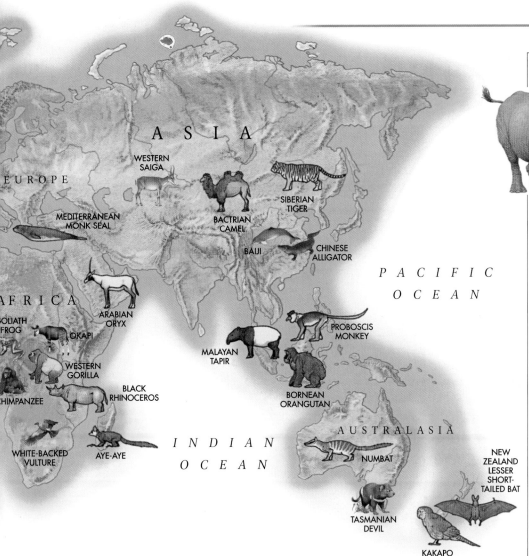

A S I A

EUROPE

WESTERN
SAIGA

MEDITERRANEAN
MONK SEAL

BACTRIAN
CAMEL

SIBERIAN
TIGER

BAIJI

CHINESE
ALLIGATOR

P A C I F I C
O C E A N

AFRICA

GOLIATH
FROG

OKAPI

ARABIAN
ORYX

WESTERN
GORILLA

CHIMPANZEE

BLACK
RHINOCEROS

MALAYAN
TAPIR

PROBOSCIS
MONKEY

BORNEAN
ORANGUTAN

WHITE-BACKED
VULTURE

AYE-AYE

I N D I A N
O C E A N

A U S T R A L A S I A

NUMBAT

NEW
ZEALAND
LESSER
SHORT-
TAILED BAT

TASMANIAN
DEVIL

KAKAPO

WHAT WE CAN DO TO HELP

Black
rhinoceros

• Stop buying goods made from rare animals, such as fur coats, skin bags and shoes, ivory carvings, or shell jewelry.
• Set aside areas of land or water as national parks or wildlife sanctuaries, where animals can live safely with as little disturbance as possible.
• Breed endangered animals in captivity in zoos or wild animal parks. This is especially important in places where it is not possible to save the animals' habitat from being destroyed. Captive-bred animals could be released back into the wild in the future if a suitable home is found.
• Pass laws against hunting rare species.
• Reduce the amount of pollution, so that animals are not killed or harmed by poisonous materials in the environment.
• Take care of the countryside by keeping to paths, taking litter home, and being careful not to disturb wild animals.
• Stop animals, such as parrots, from being taken from the wild and sold as pets.
• Join conservation organizations to protest against the things that threaten the survival of rare animals, raise money for projects, and make other people more aware of the problems.
• Carry out research to find out as much as possible about the natural lives of rare animals so that we can plan the best way to protect them.

Galápagos giant tortoise

INTRODUCED SPECIES

People take animals from one country to another. Some of these introduced species are not suited to their new home and die out. Others flourish and increase in numbers, upsetting the balance of life among animals already living in the country. On the Galápagos Islands, for instance, introduced goats compete with the native giant tortoises and land iguanas for food. Flightless birds in New Zealand, such as the kakapo, are endangered because cats, rats, stoats, and ferrets—all of which are introduced species—eat the birds' eggs and young.

Some species are introduced to a country to solve one problem but end up causing much more serious problems. Cane toads were introduced to Australia to eat beetles that were destroying the sugar cane crop. With no natural enemies in Australia, these poisonous toads spread fast, and now threaten the survival of native frogs, reptiles, and small mammals.

Osprey

POLLUTION

Many farmers use chemicals on their crops, which can seep into the soil and rivers and may poison wildlife. Poisonous chemicals from factories and sewage works may also be dumped into rivers or the sea. Another form of pollution, acid rain, is caused when the chemicals from vehicle exhausts, power stations, and factories join up with water in the air and fall as rain. Rainwater collects in streams and rivers and flows into lakes, making their waters more acidic and killing the fish that live there. Birds such as ospreys eat the fish and suffer because the poisons become concentrated in their bodies. If they ingest certain pesticides, they may lay eggs with thin shells, and have chicks with deformed bones. Acid rain also destroys forests, particularly conifer trees, reducing the habitats available for animals. Plastic pollution has become a particular concern in recent years. Plastic items are not easily broken down in the environment, and they often end up in the oceans and freshwater habitats, killing many of the seabirds and other marine animals that try to eat them..

Farmers have introduced large herds of grazing animals, such as sheep and cattle, to the grassy pampas plains of South America. Farmers often start fires to encourage the growth of new grass.

Large herds of deer once grazed on the pampas, but their range has shrunk by up to 99 per cent. A conservation program has helped to prevent their extinction.

Oil sometimes escapes into the sea after a tanker runs aground. Oil sticks birds' feathers together, so they cannot keep out the cold and wet or dive for food.

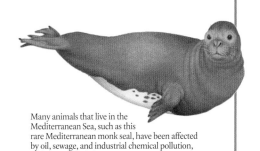

Many animals that live in the Mediterranean Sea, such as this rare Mediterranean monk seal, have been affected by oil, sewage, and industrial chemical pollution, making it difficult for some species to survive.

INDEX

A

acid rain 63
addax 35
albatross, wandering 59, 60
alligator
  American 16
  Chinese 49, 63
alpaca 23
amphibians 5
anemone, giant carpet 56
ant
  trap-jaw 18
  wood 28
anteater, giant 27
antelope, royal 36
armadillo
  giant 25
  pink fairy 26
ass, Asiatic wild 44
aye-aye 40

B

badger, European 30
baiji 48, 63
bat
  brown long-eared 28
  Kitti's hog-nosed 51, 60
  short-tailed 58
  vampire 18
bear
  brown 32
  grizzly 12
  Himalayan black 47
  spectacled 47
bearded vulture
  see lammergeyer
beaver, North American 11
beetle
  Caspian darkling 45
  European stag 30
  golden scarab 19
  goliath 60
  sacred scarab 35
bilby, greater 52
bird of paradise, Raggiana 55
birds 5
bluebird, mountain 13
boa, emerald tree 25
bobcat 12
booby, blue-footed 21
Brazilian guinea pig 27
bunting, painted 17
bustard, great 45
butterfly
  Bhutan glory 46
  desert swallowtail 14
  monarch 11
  Queen Alexandra's birdwing 55, 60
  rhetenor blue morpho 24
  Rocky Mountain parnassian 12
  zebra 16

C

caiman 62
  spectacled 24
camel
  bactrian 44
  dromedary 35
capercaillie, western 29
caracara, southern 26
caribou see reindeer
cat
  Pallas's 45
  sand 34
  wild 28
chameleon 61
  Parson's 41
chamois, Alpine 32
cheetah 38, 60
chimpanzee 37, 63
chinchilla, Chilean 23
chipmunk, least 10
clam, giant 56
clownfish 56
cobra, king 50
coelacanth 41
colugo 51
condor, Andean 22
coral, orange cup 56
coral reef 7, 56
cormorant, flightless 20
cottonmouth 16
cougar see lion, mountain
crab, sally lightfoot 20
crane, whooping 10
crossbill, red 28
crown-of-thorns starfish 56

D

Darwin, Charles 20
deer
  common fallow 30
  forest musk 49
  pampas 26, 63
  sika 48
  western red 29
deserts 7
  African 34
  American 14
  Asian 44
  Australian 52
dingo 53
dormouse, hazel 31
dragon, Komodo 51
duck
  common eider 9
  torrent 23

E

eagle
  bald 11
  harpy 25
  steppe 44
echidna, short-beaked 52
elephant
  African savannah 38, 60
  Asian 50
emu 52

F

falcon
  peregrine 60
  sooty 35
fer-de-lance 18
finch, woodpecker 21
fish 5
  blue-streaked cleaner wrasse 56
  ocean sunfish 60
  threadfin butterflyfish 56
flamingo, greater 33
flea, common 60
flicker, Andean 23
flycatcher, little vermilion 21
forests 6
  American 10
  Asian 42, 48, 50
  European 28
fosa 40
fox
  Arctic 8
  fennec 34
  kit 14
  red 31
frog
  Darwin's 22, 62
  goliath 37, 63
  green tree 17
  Hamilton's 58
  Panamanian golden 18
  water-holding 53
frigate bird, magnificent 21

G

gar, long-nosed 17
gazelle
  yarkand 45
  Thomson's 39
gecko, leaf-tailed 55
genet, common 33
gila monster 15
giraffe 39, 60
glider, sugar 54
goat, Rocky Mountain 13
gorilla, western 36, 62
grassland 6
  African 38
  American 10, 26
  Asian 44
ground tyrant, dark-faced 22
grouse
  hazel 43
  sage 10
guinea pig, Brazilian 27

H

hamster, common 44
hare
  mountain 9
  snowshoe 12
hedgehog
  desert 34
  west European 31
hippopotamus 37
hoatzin 24
honey bear see kinkajou
hoopoe, common 32
hornbill, black-casqued 37
hummingbird
  bee 18, 60
  giant 23
  ruby-topaz 25
hyena, spotted 38

I

ibex, Siberian 46
ibis, scarlet 19
ichneumon, giant 29
iguana
  land 20, 63
  marine 21
indri 41
invertebrates 5

J

jacana, African 37
jackrabbit, black-tailed 15
jaguar 24
jay
  blue 11
  Siberian 43
jerboa 34
  long-eared 45

K

kakapo 58, 63
kangaroo
  Goodfellow's tree 54
  red 53
kea 58
kinkajou 18
kite, snail 16
kiwi, northern brown 58
koala 55
kookaburra, blue-winged 55
krill, Antarctic 59

L

ladybug, two-spotted 10
lammergeyer 32
langur, Hanuman 46
lemming, Siberian 43
lemur
  flying see colugo
  ring-tailed 40
leopard 36, 62
  snow 46
lily-trotter see jacana, African
lion 39
lizard
  common collared 15
  desert monitor 44
  frilled 52
  North African spiny-tailed 35
lorikeet, rainbow 54
lynx, Iberian 33, 62

M

macaque
  Barbary 33
  Japanese 48
macaw, scarlet 25
mallee fowl 52
mammals 5
manatee, West Indian 17
mara, Patagonian 26
markhor 47
marmot, Himalayan 47
marshland 7, 16
mayfly 61
Mediterranean 6, 32, 63
mole, marsupial 53
monkey
  black spider 24
  proboscis 51
  ursine red howler 19, 61
moose 10
mosquito 17
moth, atlas 50
mountains 7
  American 12, 22
  Asian 46
mudskipper, gold spotted 51
mulgara, brush-tailed 53
musk ox 8
myzornis, fire-tailed 47

N

narwhal 8
numbat 55
nuthatch
  Eurasian 30
  vanga 41

O

ocelot 19
okapi 36, 63
olm 32
onager see ass, Asiatic wild
opossum, Virginia 11
orangutan, Bornean 51
oriole, Eurasian golden 33
osprey 28
ostrich 60
ounce see leopard, snow
ovenbird 27
owl
  burrowing 27
  northern long-eared 28
  snowy 43
  tawny 31

P

pademelon, rufous-bellied 57
pampas 6, 26, 63
panda
  giant 48
  red 49
pangolin, common
  African 36
parrot 61
  ground 57
  owl see kakapo
  St. Vincent Amazon 19, 62
peafowl, blue 51
pelican, brown 16
penguin
  Emperor 59
  Galápagos 21
perentie 52
pheasant
  blood 46
  golden 48
pig
  bush 41
  European wild 30
pine marten, European 29
piranha 61
  red 25
plankton 8
platypus 57, 61
polar regions 6, 8, 59
polar bear 8
polecat 29
porcupine, North American 12
possum, honey 55
prairie dog, black-tailed 11
prairies 6, 10
ptarmigan, white-tailed 13
pudu, southern 22
puma 13

Q R

quetzal, resplendent 19, 60
quoll, spotted-tailed 57
raccoon 10
rainforest 7
  African 36
  American 24
  Asian 50
  Australasian 54
rattlesnake, western diamondback 14
reindeer 43
reptiles 5
rhea, greater 26
rhinoceros 62
  black 39
  Indian 50
roadrunner 14

S

sable 43
saiga, western 45, 63
salamander
  cave see olm
  Japanese giant 49
sandgrouse, Lichenstein's 35
savannah 6, 38
scorpion, desert 34
scrubland 6, 32, 50
seal
  Baikal 42
  bearded 8
  Galápagos fur 21
  hooded 8
  leopard 59
  Mediterranean monk 33, 63
  southern elephant 59
sheep
  Barbary 35
  bighorn 12
shrew, common tree 48
sifaka, Verreaux's 40
skink, blue-tongued 53
skunk 61
  western spotted 14
sloth, three-toed 25, 60
snail, giant African 37
snake, egg-eating 61
solenodon, Cuban 19
spider
  black widow 61
  Sydney funnel-web 54
spinebill, western 54
spoonbill, roseate 17
squirrel
  Arctic ground 43
  Eurasian red 31
  northern flying 13
  relict ground 45
steppe 6, 44
stick insect 41
sunbird-asity, common 40
swamp 7
  American 16, 18
  Asian 50
swan, whooper 42

T

taiga 6
taipan 54
takin 47
tapir
  Malayan 50
  mountain 22
tarantula, desert 15
Tasmanian devil 57, 63
tenrec, tail-less 40
termite 60
  South Africa 38
tern, Arctic 9, 61
thorny devil 53
thread-wing ant-lion 33
thylacine 57
tiger, Siberian 49
tinamou, elegant crested 27
tit
  Eurasian blue 30
  Siberian 43
toad
  cane 63
  green 32
tortoise
  Agassiz's desert 15
  giant 21, 63
toucan, red-billed 24
tuatara 58, 61
tundra 6, 42
turtle, loggerhead 16, 62

V

varan see lizard, desert monitor
vicuna 22
viper
  gaboon 36
  lebetine 44
viscacha, plains 26
vulture
  Himalayan griffon 47
  white-backed 39, 63

WYZ

walrus 9
wapiti 13
warble-fly, reindeer 8
waxwing, Bohemian 42
weasel, least 31
weaver bird, red-headed 39
whale
  beluga 9
  blue 59, 60
wildebeest, blue 38
wolf, gray 42
  maned 27
  Tasmanian see thylacine
wolverine 11
wombat, southern hairy-nosed 53
woodlands 6
  American 10
  Australasian 54
  European 30
woodpecker
  gila 15
  great spotted 31
wren, cactus 14
yak 47
zebra, Burchell's 38

ACKNOWLEDGMENTS

Dorling Kindersley would like to thank the following:
Rachel Foster and David Gillingwater for additional design help; Struan Reid and Kathakali Banerjee for editorial assistance; Anita Yadav for DTP assistance; Lynn Bresler for compiling the index; Jessica Cawthra for proofreading; and Aziz Khan for the maps.

Picture Credits
The publisher would like to thank the following for their kind permission to reproduce their photographs:
(Key: a-above; b-below/bottom; c-centre; f-far; l-left; r-right; t-top)

1 Ardea: Roger Hall / Science Source (bl). **5 Getty Images:** De Agostini Picture Library (cr); Encyclopaedia Britannica/UIG (cla). **6 Depositphotos Inc:** KSponsler (cl). **Dorling Kindersley:** Sawgrass Recreation Park (cra). **Dreamstime.com:** Gabriel Rojo (crb); Toldiu74 (cr). **7 Dreamstime.com:** Beijada (ca); Th9515 (cr); Aliaksandr Mazurkevich (cb); Kiyoshi Hijiki (crb); Staphy (bc). **9 Dreamstime.com:** Polina Bublik (ca); Natalia Golubnycha (cr); Martinmark (cb). **10 Dreamstime.com:** Jarett Stein (crb); Kelly Vandellen (br). **11 Dreamstime.com:** Joe Sohm (cl). **13 Depositphotos Inc:** klevit.shaw.ca (clb). **Dreamstime.com:** Sherry Young (c). **15 Dreamstime.com:** Wollertz (cla); Jakub Zajic (tc). **Getty Images:** Encyclopaedia Britannica / UIG (cb); De Agostini Picture Library (c). **16 Alamy Stock Photo:** philipus (crb). **Ardea:** Roger Hall / Science Source (tr). **17 Dreamstime.com:** Giovanni Gagliardi (c); Littleny (bl). **18 Science Photo Library:** Jim Smith (cra). **19 Dreamstime.com:** Claudio Bruni (cb); Irstone (bl). **20 Dreamstime.com:** Donyanedomam (cla); Natursports (cla); Irina Gomelsky (ca). **23 Dreamstime.com:** Kseniya Ragozina (cra, crb); Toniflap (tr). **24 Dreamstime.com:** Ulf Huebner (crb). **25 Dreamstime.com:** Jekaterina Sahmanova (bl); Aleksandr Vorobev (bc). **27 Depositphotos Inc:** FOTO4440 (cl/Map). **Dreamstime.**

com: Iakov Filimonov (cl); Sergio Schnitzler (tl). **29 Dreamstime.com:** Pablo Hidalgo (cr); Teemu Tretjakov (clb); Dmitry Naumov (br). **30 Dreamstime.com:** Adrian Szatewicz (crb). **31 Dreamstime.com:** Bjornforenius (cb); Martin Graf (cl). **32 Depositphotos Inc:** ihervas (br). **33 Dreamstime.com:** Gornostaj (cb); Prillfoto (cl). **34 Dreamstime.com:** Lukasz Janyst (crb); Dmitry Pichugin (c). **35 Alamy Stock Photo:** Publishing Group LLC Azbooka-Atticus/dieKleinert (cla). **Dreamstime.com:** Dagobert1620 (cl). **37 Dreamstime.com:** Frans Lanting / Frans Lanting Studio (clb). **Dreamstime.com:** Flytraveler (bc); Christian Weiß (crb). **39 Dreamstime.com:** Andreanita (clb); Isselee (cl); Grantotufo (clb/Acacias). **41 Alamy Stock Photo:** International Photobank (tr). **Depositphotos Inc:** pawopa3336 (ca). **Dreamstime.com:** Artushfoto (tr). **Dreamstime.com:** Iuliia Kuzenkova (clb); Mao Mao (bl). **45 Dreamstime.com:** Dimaberkut (ca); Aleksandr Frolov (crb); Aleksandr Katarzhin (clb). **46 Dreamstime.com:** Axel2001

(br); Lsprasath (bc). **47 Dreamstime.com:** Mubarak Khan (bl). **49 Dreamstime.com:** Jingaiping (cl); Wenbin Yu (tc); Askar Karimullin (ca). **51 123RF.com:** Kristine Sergejeva (tl). **Dreamstime.com:** Puntasit Choksawatdikorn (cla); FootageLab (cl). **52 Dreamstime.com:** Mark Higgins (cb). **53 Dreamstime.com:** Pavel Šťastný (clb). **54 Dreamstime.com:** Martin Valigursky (c). **naturepl.com:** Gerry Ellis (cra); Jurgen Freund (cb). **56 Dreamstime.com:** Lizgiv (bl); Whitcomberd (clb). **Getty Images:** Daniel Osterkamp (cb). **57 Dreamstime.com:** Ryszard Stelmachowicz (cr). **58 Dreamstime.com:** BiancoBlue (c); Miu861 (cb); Dmitry Pichugin / Dmitryp (bl). **59 Dreamstime.com:** Adfoto (bc, br); Darryn Schneider (crb). **62 Alamy Stock Photo:** Balonicici (bc/Fur coats). **63 Alamy Stock Photo:** Javier Larrea/Age fotostock (tr). **iStockphoto.com:** Edsel Querini/E+ (bl)

All other images © Dorling Kindersley
For further information see: www.dkimages.com